The Real Brass Ring

....

Change Your Life Course Now!

DIANNE BISCHOFF JAMES

TURNING
STONE
PRESS

First published in 2013 by
Turning Stone Press, an imprint of
Red Wheel/Weiser, LLC
With offices at:
665 Third Street, Suite 400
San Francisco, CA 94107
www.redwheelweiser.com

ISBN: 978-1-61852-055-5

Cover design by Jim Warner

Printed in the United States of America
IBT
10 9 8 7 6 5 4 3 2 1

Contents

SECTION I

Midway on Life's Journey and on the Wrong Path

*Sonia stood up, leaned forward, and whispered a final note
of caution to me: "Change your course now, Dianne. Fix
your ways, or soon it will be too late."*

*When I wasn't building my business, I cared for the kids,
serving the family from sunup to sundown. I was fat and
depressed, and my husband acted a lot more like a girlfriend
than a soul mate. This was my reality.*

*"I will rediscover my passion, leaving nothing repressed or
undone. I will re-create myself: lose weight, perform in the
theater, improve my relationship, journal my stories, and
find a career to help others grow. I will fulfill these dreams!"*

*I'm not the kind of person who typically believes in ghosts,
but I walked straight into the middle of the living room to
address the situation directly. I spoke with imposing volume
and waved my arms to demonstrate complete authority. "I'm
telling you to stop haunting us, walking up stairs, opening
doors, and turning things on and off."*

*In my spare time, I developed a training program to help
people manifest their true desires. Now, I just needed to find
a willing lab partner, someone who was open and receptive
to a powerful new way of thinking. It was 2003 and several
years before* The Secret *popularized New Age concepts, so
finding a student wasn't particularly easy.*

Modern Family, Secret Separation

*Everyone knew therapy wasn't going to solve our marital
problem. We didn't have that kind of money, and Rob and I
didn't have what it took for a husband-and-wife relationship,
period, end of story. We left knowing change was imminent.*

*Over the next few months, I established a rare and fasci-
nating double life. By day, I was a focused, hardworking
suburban mother of three. By night, I was a single woman
experiencing the pulse of one of the world's liveliest cities.*

*I took a hard look at my materialistic choices. I'd naively
thought my financial abundance would continue forever; I
believed the economy would improve. My own desire for possessions had led me to a terrifying financial cliff.*

In retrospect, the past decade was an organic voyage, each event emerging without structure or order. I took the roller-coaster ride from middle income to wealth to poverty, from fat to fit, from a mountain of lies to truth, from a broken body to strength, and from a loveless connection to standing side by side with a soul mate.

Preface

A Journey of Reinvention

I wrote the *Real Brass Ring* over a ten-year period on a tiny Victorian piano desk that was shoved into the back corner of our house. There, I recorded a personal story filled with many Universal lessons. It was written through a myriad of personal challenges, divorce, waves of economic decline, physical aches and pain, and tears. During the day, I did my best to earn a living and tend to the needs of my three children. From midnight until two a.m., I forced myself to hit the keyboard.

The entire voyage was an organic journey, an unstructured process that was completely unfamiliar to me. The words also didn't come easily. They flowed like a river, randomly starting and stopping across both charted and uncharted land.

I didn't compose the manuscript because I wanted to. Often times, I imagined myself with a whip and a chair. I was my own lion tamer, poking and prodding the little girl inside who just wanted to sit and watch TV or take a walk down the street. Yet, there was a driving force that compelled me to articulate the minute details of my life's transition post-forty. "Get back on the computer and keep on typing!" bellowed the voice within my mind-space. "Don't ask yourself if you 'want' to write it. You don't get to ask that question. You have to!" Slave-driver girl would not let me opt-out or quit because there was a gnawing unrest that lay beneath my breastbone and it grew larger and stronger as the years passed, becoming too great to ignore.

At the same time, I was burdened with shame and doubt. In midlife, I'd opened Pandora's Box, the raw, ugly truth hidden behind the well-crafted, ornate parade that I called "my life." I loathed the contents. I was not proud of myself or of what I'd accomplished. Instead, I was horrified and ashamed of the lies surrounding my big house, marriage, and the monstrously false trappings of the North Shore. This was not me. I inch-wormed my way through the muck. I stood toe-to-toe, facing the most powerful of all questions, "Who am I and what did I come here to do in this lifetime?"

Without an answer for the first half of my life, I'd truly morphed into a flaccid societal mannequin, following rules my soul had never agreed to. I only wish I'd had the courage to expose the cover-ups that coated my heart throughout my early years. But it took me until forty to grant myself permission to self-reveal and expose the raw personal truths. And now, my path can exemplify the fact that no matter how hard or how long it takes, it's never too late to become a successful Midlife Reinventionist.

While approaching the end of my writing process, my eldest daughter asked me, "So Mom, what is the 'real brass ring'?" The answer erupted like a volcano spewing ash across the surrounding land. The "real brass ring" is our world filled with endless possibilities. I explained that the ring starts to form when you know yourself well and understand what brings you joy. Eventually, it solidifies with a focused vision and an open expression of your clear desires, even if others tell you it can't be done. And finally, when an opportunity arrives, you need to grab the brass ring with all of your might. The ring might not come in a traditional package, so be ready to climb in the "window" and not the door because even the smallest step forward will make you feel happier and align you more closely with your greatest potential.

If this book can help in any way to remind you that your future is lined with infinite possibilities and the middle years can be the greatest time of your life, then it will have accomplished its purpose. And, I will celebrate with you in my heart.

Acknowledgments

I would like to acknowledge the young woman who kept me motivated over the many years it took to develop this book. I would like to honor the individual who assured me that in the end my efforts would not be in vain. I would like to thank with eternal appreciation the glorious soul who encouraged me to keep going despite mountainous fears and doubt. And, I greatly admire her courage and willingness into share the sensitive experiences of our past so that others may possibly relate, learn, and grow.

I dedicate my heart-felt journey to Alexandra, my beautifully spiritual daughter, who is an open channel for all that is good in this world.

With love and much gratitude,
Mom

~

SECTION I

*Midway On Life's Journey
and On the Wrong Path*

~

☙ 1 ❧

Outed by a Psychic

Sonia stood up, leaned forward, and whispered a final note of caution to me: "Change your course now, Dianne. Fix your ways, or soon it will be too late."

∽

I'll always remember February 6, 2000, because it was my thirty-eighth birthday and the day I gave myself an expensive gift, a reading with world-renowned psychic Sonia Choquette.

I arrived at Sonia's home office both nervous and excited, expecting to hear words of great promise and praise for my life filled with marvelous accomplishments. After all, I had what everyone wanted: a profitable marketing business, a house in the high-rent district, a long-term marriage, two small children, a cat, a dog, and a fish. I was a supercharged helicopter parent and a business professional with well-groomed skills in marketing and advertising. Surely, this intuitive woman would paint a picture of my future as rosy and bright.

I took a seat in the waiting room and stared at colorful oversized posters that lined the walls featuring Sonia's literary work: metaphysical books woven around the topic of trusting your vibes. I nervously wrung my hands and chatted with her assistant, Ryan. We spoke about her international publicity tour and certification training course. It was all quite impressive.

When the clock struck ten, the enthusiastic young man hopped up and led me into the inner sanctum, a cozy private office filled from floor to ceiling with whimsical paintings, eclectic gadgets, and a slew of New Age books. Sonia entered, tall, thin, and fresh-faced, without a trace of makeup, as if she had just woken up. She greeted me with an impish, childlike grin.

I sat down at a small circular table and watched with curiosity as she pulled out a deck of tarot cards decorated with vibrant Gothic imagery. She pushed them in my direction and instructed me to shuffle the deck so I could become more "grounded," as she put it. Then she grabbed an old, tattered astrology book and dropped her face down low, carefully studying the planetary data surrounding my date of birth.

Suddenly, she jerked up and shook her tight russet curls back and forth. The silence was broken. Sonia spoke in a robotic fashion, as if the information was being downloaded. "Dianne, you are a talented writer, healer, teacher, and performer. But regrettably, your life is heading down the wrong path." She paused and cast her brown eyes upon my face. "Your brass ring is coming by and you need to grab it before it's too late. You've modeled yourself after your parents' desires. You're completely stuck in the make-believe role of being a 'good girl' and you live with depression because nothing about your life is your own."

My fingers dug deep into the plush armrest. A surging pulse throbbed through my veins. She continued aggressively, "You are standing directly in your own way and not following your purpose. You are like an unlit Christmas tree; none of your bulbs are firing. You're here on this planet to help people become more aware of their own abilities and find their given course."

She marched on with a tidal wave of personal critiques: "You're overly burdened by the role of being a parent, and yet you smother your children. Instead of finding support, you've mastered the art of not needing anything from anyone. You really don't have any true friends, people whom you can consider peers. But the most disconcerting part is, you came here to find your heart, this being one of the most difficult of all Earthly lessons. Unfortunately, your marriage is fraternal and this, my dear, is not a true heart connection." I sank even lower into the chair and felt a constriction in my chest as if I were being suffocated.

Her psychic barrage continued. She commanded, "Go back to the stage. You will make a nice name for yourself in acting and theater. Write a little bit every day, because the world will benefit from your stories. Build a strong foundation for a successful public life. Go to the Hoffman Institute to release the stubborn childhood patterns that have led you astray. I'll give you a list of books at the end of our session. Read them and expand your understanding of the world. Also, schedule a session with my husband. He's a massage therapist and can help you manage the body issues you're currently developing."

Sonia stood up, leaned forward, and whispered a final note of caution to me. "Change your course now, Dianne. Fix your ways, or soon it will be too late."

As she turned to run out the doorway, I squeaked out a single burning question, "What happens if I don't find my heart?"

Sonia spun around and quipped, "Then you have to come back and do it all over again!" In a flash, she was gone.

I put on my coat and gloves and walked unsteadily onto the snowy sidewalk in a state of post-traumatic shock. I yanked open the icy car door and sat down inside, fumbling, trying to shove the keys into the ignition of my now frozen vehicle. I shuddered uncontrollably, spouting tears that soaked my red leather gloves. I sat there, alone, crying and shivering on my blustery birthday for what seemed like hours, shaken to the core. Sonia had peered into the desolate, shadowy corners of my soul. She had seen my unspoken terrors and detailed every aspect of my faulty life.

This soft-spoken woman had put me through a penetrating "Life Review." She inventoried my secrets and exposed all the lies. Then, she neatly piled them up like freshly folded laundry and swung her bat. On the outside, my résumé looked perfect, with a busy household, entrepreneurial career, and long-term marriage, but at the subterranean level, it was a grand personal charade. My entire adult existence was a sham.

After such a personal attack, I couldn't help but self-righteously blame the messenger. "I hate her! Who does she think she is? How could she say those things to me?" I screamed loudly, hitting my fists on the steering wheel as my heavy breath steamed up the windows. My brain was racing: *I'm thirty-eight years old. How can I be going down the wrong road? Did I really miss the brass ring? Why didn't I see it coming? Oh God, I'm a total failure!*

I swallowed hard, thrusting my heaving emotions back down inside where they belonged. I used a finger to wipe underneath my swollen eyes in an attempt to repair the smudged makeup. I had a client meeting in the city in less than an hour. I sniffed back the weepiness and reassured myself, "I'll tell my clients I have allergies." Forcing analytical thoughts back into my brain, I drove onto the snow-covered street. After all, I was a dedicated business professional.

❧ 2 ❧

Stinking Thinking

*When I wasn't building my business, I cared for the kids,
serving the family from sunup to sundown. I was fat and
depressed, and my husband acted a lot more like a girlfriend than a soul mate. This was my reality.*

❧

I'd followed my parents' instructions for structuring
a winning life. As a child I listened intently to their
career selection guidelines: "Be a doctor, lawyer, engi-
neer, or accountant so that you can have some fundamental skills on which you can rely!" Well, I guess my
two siblings had also been listening to these sage direc-
tions, because guess what? My older brother had become
a state's attorney, my younger brother had become an
emergency room physician, and as the family rebel, I had
become a business marketing professional.

Congratulations! We all hated our careers. My elder
brother jumped ship and quit law after ten years to join
an international auction house for antiques and collect-
ibles. My younger brother maintained a grueling medical

career, but after working the ER graveyard shift for so many years, he could barely function during daylight hours. And I was bored to death, talking all day to engineers about jumper cables, gadgets, and deep-water drilling equipment.

When I wasn't building my business, I cared for the kids, serving the family from sunup to sundown. I was fat and depressed, and my husband acted a lot more like a girlfriend than a soul mate. This was my reality.

The worst part was, I felt nothing on the inside but immeasurable sorrow. I'd followed my parents' formula of a high-end career, suburban life, private schools, and weekends spent toting kids to volleyball and ballet. But this part is true: Busy doesn't buy you happiness; it just buys you exhaustion. It took a skinny psychic with pixie-like curls to catch me red-handed in a gigantic, handcrafted farce.

Most days, I woke up in a fog of lethargy and fatigue. I dragged myself out of bed, trudging up an endless mountain of "to dos." Day in and day out, I had invisible dogs nipping at my heels barking, *Do more! Move faster! Work harder! Make more money! Spend more time with the kids! And stop eating so much!* All the while, my gut churned with wrenching, repressed anguish.

As Sonia had revealed, over the past two decades I had done my best to manage an ominous gray cloud of depression that perpetually hovered over my head. Throughout my twenties, I felt tired, weary, even despondent, but I drank coffee and ate candy to counteract the problem. I used sugar and caffeine to accelerate my sticky, slow blood cells so I wouldn't feel down-in-the-dumps. I worked to harness the heavy fog of indolence and hopelessness. I kept my body in motion so I wouldn't touch base with what was really going on.

As I got older, my depression grew in depth and breadth. By the time I was married and delivered my first child, the "blues barometer" hit an all-time low. I couldn't control the raw, pervasive sensation of misery. I cried spontaneously, even at work. Acknowledging something was seriously wrong with me, I sought medical attention. Rather than review my health history or even give me a physical exam, the doctor handed me a yearlong prescription for Prozac.

Finally, I had a drug that would raise my waning serotonin. Surely this mood-altering chemical would make me feel cheery and give me back a smile. While taking the popular antidepressant, I functioned with Stepford-like efficiency, completing work and child-care duties in a fast, orderly fashion. Prozac was like emotional Botox. I had no feelings whatsoever, but after dealing with depression for so long it was a miraculous relief.

I'd been on Prozac for nearly ten months when we experienced a death in the family. My mother and I attended my cousin's wake, the saddest event I'd ever witnessed. I sat in the pew like a glass toad, eyes wide open, looking objectively to the right and left at a church filled with sobbing mourners. When it was time to pay my respects, I walked over to my cousin and stared at her pale, waxen face in the open casket. I felt absolutely nothing: no grief, no sorrow, not even a twinge of compassion. While driving home from the funeral that evening I acknowledged the truth: I'd become a Lidocaine shell of a human being, numbed to the point of emptiness. By medicating myself, I'd traded depression for an emotional void. The very next day, I stopped popping the magic "happy pill," cold turkey. I knew I had to experience my authentic self once again, even if I felt bad.

A week after my appointment with Sonia, the shock from the verbal slaying had subsided, but the gravity of her words lay heavy on my heart: "Change your course now!" The warning festered and grew in the pit of my stomach. Sonia was right. Every area of my life was wrong: mind, body, work, parenting, marriage, and friends. I needed a complete life overhaul. I was sitting between two worlds: the stale, boring, tedious world modeled for me in childhood and the creative, vibrant, exhilarating world of my dreams.

The notion of transformational change, however, was chock-full of profound implications. How do I lose weight, break into the acting business, fix my marriage, find real friends, and start a career as a teacher and healer? I had to face the facts: I was a drained, weary marketer who wrote technical brochures about product testing, insurance, and medical devices. *What the bleep do I do now?*

Overwhelmed by the magnitude of my impending personal renovation, I decided to do the only easy thing on the list. I picked up the phone and called Sonia's husband, Patrick, for a massage therapy appointment.

Patrick was a tall, slender man with penetrating azure eyes; everything about him was soothing, from his soft baritone voice to his strong, kneading touch. A session with him was the ideal remedy for my pervasive stress. With my head propped in the massage cradle, Patrick dug underneath my shoulder blades and I uncontrollably spewed forth the details of my psychic stabbing. After all, he was married to this chick, so he must have been accustomed to post-session rants.

Patrick listened intently until my tale came to an end. Then, he posed a profound question: "Tell me, Dianne, what did you come here to do this lifetime?"

I searched for an analytical response. I paused, sputtering and spurting as my sinuses filled with gravity congestion. I had no answer. I spoke softly toward the floor, "I'm not sure."

I felt so ashamed. I should've had a well-developed postulate to deliver. Patrick wanted to hear my personal mission: a description of what I came here to do. After all, isn't that the most important of all universal questions? I wanted to spin a clever narrative to make him believe I was a sharp, intelligent woman on a deliberate and clear expedition. But instead, I impetuously spit out an early memory. It was a vision from when I was ten years old and somehow it seemed relevant.

"I remember when I was little, sitting in my room on a fluffy pink beanbag chair, too lazy to move, when an image appeared to me. I saw a woman, a public speaker walking energetically up a set of silver stairs that led to an enthusiastic audience. She opened her arms and greeted a welcoming crowd. The lights hit her shoulder-length hair as she sauntered toward center stage and took a grand bow. I squinted hard, trying to focus on her face. Slowly it came into view and I screamed. The woman was a much older version of me, as old as my mother. I still think about that daydream because it seemed so real. Perhaps my mission is somehow tied to it."

Patrick continued to probe. "What was the vision supposed to show you?"

I responded with the first notion that popped into my mushy, massaged head. "I think I'm here to help others get what they want out of life. Wait a minute. Maybe I do have a mission after all!"

As soon as the massage appointment was finished, I quickly dressed, tamed my Medusa-like hair, and trotted to the car. I sat outside Sonia's home on yet another freezing morning, but this time my eyes were dry. I grabbed a piece of paper from the glove compartment and wrote down the significant nuggets from our weighty discussion. Whether I liked it or not, this dynamic couple had set me sailing on a journey that would alter my life forever. With one hand on the wheel and the other holding tightly on to the notepaper, I drove off to pitch my marketing services to a new client.

That night, I sat at my computer and crafted a mission by which I could strategically live. I edited the verbiage until a cohesive statement beamed forth:

Dianne's Personal Mission: I came here to help others find and achieve their greatest good by finding and achieving my own.

I read it over and over. The words sounded lofty and inspiring, but what does an analytically minded business professional do with such esoteric mumbo jumbo? Who was I kidding? I didn't help people find their greatest good. I was just a working mom with a plate full of kids, clients, and millions of chores.

At the midpoint of my life, I had a clear understanding of what was wrong, but no idea how to fix it. *How do I start on a journey of course correction?* It would've been helpful to have had a guidebook or organizational plan, but much to my chagrin, I had nothing. So I did the next best thing . . . I ordered Sonia's recommended reading materials.

I discovered my first New Age book at the tender age of twelve, devouring Shirley MacLaine's *Dancing in the Light.*

Along the path of my spiritual search, I felt a longing more and more to understand *why* I had lived before and what I could learn in the present incarnation in relation to those past lives. For me, it was as Einstein said: "Knowledge is really nothing but experience." I wanted the experience. Since each of us *is what we are consciously aware of,* I wanted to become aware of more. I was intensely curious as to what raising my consciousness might reveal to my higher unlimited self.

—Shirley MacLaine, *Dancing in the Light*

I became obsessed with MacLaine's enlightened manuscript, innately curious about what my higher unlimited self could learn in this present incarnation. Despite the fact that I was born into a family with an active Catholic lineage, attended parochial schools, received all the sacraments, and had an uncle who served as archbishop of Kansas City, Catholicism was not for me. As a youngster, I became hooked on metaphysics and intent on understanding what we're supposed to achieve while here on Earth.

I continued my pursuit with an undergraduate degree in both psychology and philosophy, learning about human behavior and profound historical ideologies. I practiced Transcendental Meditation to master my thoughts. I studied *A Course in Miracles* to absorb the heady ego-versus-essence doctrine. I took an Avatar class to unlock my subconscious reactionary emotional responses, and for a year, I climbed aboard Scientology's "bridge" as a Thetan.

And although I've read almost every self-help book ever written, the psychic told me to read more, so I did. I started with Sonia's book *Your Heart's Desire,* which describes the process for allowing intuition to guide us through life. I then moved on to Harville Hendrix's *Getting the Love You Want*, a dynamic paradigm for finding love; *The Power of Now*, Eckhart Tolle's journey into the art of "being"; and David Schnarch's *Passionate Marriage*, which focuses on techniques for keeping intimacy alive.

The content, however, that really rocked my boat was found in three small pamphlets written by Esther and Jerry Hicks: *The Law of Attraction*, *The Law of Mutual Creation*, and *The Law of Allowing*. The Hickses were new to the metaphysical scene and their tiny leaflets were filled with divinely guided doctrine that addressed man's current existential challenge. According to the "laws," human beings have come here as leading-edge creators, active partners working with Source to establish a blissful, fulfilling existence. Unfortunately, most people have faulty programming. We do not look at the world as "whole and complete." Instead, we perceive the world from a place of "lack," as if it were broken and needed to be fixed.

> We hope you are hearing the power of these words. For if you are able to grasp that our day's work, your real work, is to look around for the thing that you want, with the intent of bringing it into (your personal) workshop, in order to create your vision of self from which you will attract, then you will come to know that there is nothing that you cannot be or do or have.
>
> —Esther and Jerry Hicks, *The Law of Attraction*, A Transcription of Tape AB-2

It was true. My own worldly perceptions were defective and thought processes askew. I didn't have a personal workshop from which I could create. And I didn't believe that my limitless desires could be manifested. Driven on a quest for more knowledge, I purchased a ticket to see Esther Hicks present her material live in Chicago as part of a national Abraham-Hicks road show.

I walked straight into a hotel ballroom filled with curious onlookers. Esther, a middle-aged woman in a black blazer and with long, striped gray hair, was standing on a small skirtless stage delivering a channeled message from the pristine entity she called "Abraham." Esther spoke in an Old English dialect. "We are pleased that thou art here with us today."

Why is she talking like she's in a Shakespearean play? I thought as I sat down. Esther delivered insights from her channeled source about the enigmatic concepts of vibration, energy flow, and idea management. She explained that in order to get what we truly wanted, we had to use positive thoughts to manifest our desires and follow a stream of nonresistance.

> Most people believe that control of conditions and of others is the key to feeling better, but that belief is the greatest flawed premise of all. The belief that you could get all circumstances to change so that your observation of them would then feel good to you defies the Laws of the Universe, as well as your reason for being here. It was never your intention to control everything around you. It was your intention to control the direction of your thought.
>
> —Esther and Jerry Hicks, *The Vortex*

Esther's theory excited every cell in my body. She spoke extensively about our real work, controlling the direction of our thoughts. Clearly, I'd been doing everything wrong. It was time for me to put my head on straight, stop feeling depressed, get happy, and figure out what I came here to do or find the brass ring, whichever came first. When the lecture was over, I ran out and purchased the complete set of Abraham-Hicks cassette tapes. *I was going to sanitize my brain, fix my world, and become a master of the Law of Attraction, just like Esther.*

As a businessperson, I get excited about executive summaries, so after listening to her complete set of materials, I sat down and created a study guide with ten consumable rules based not only on Abraham-Hicks, but also on the various metaphysical practices I'd studied over the years. This was my efficient "cheat sheet," which I titled "The Shortcuts for Living Well."

The Shortcuts for Living Well

Rule 1: It's All Good

The Universe is already in order and in a state of wellbeing. We didn't come here to fix anything, because nothing is broken.

Dianne's Initial Feedback

If the world is complete and abundant, why do I keep running around trying to improve it and worrying about my next dime? Does this mean I can stop working so hard, relax, and just enjoy being here?

Rule 2: What You Think about You Bring About

We are always attracting. Everything you think about, talk about, and pay attention to is coming your way, so make it good.

<u>Dianne's Initial Feedback</u>

I've been raised by second-generation fear-based survivalists. Positive self-talk is a whole new skill set that will require tremendous practice on my part.

Rule 3: Leverage Your Alignment

When you're aligned physically, emotionally, and spiritually, you'll experience joy. Connect vibrationally with who you are so that your Earthly part, the body, joins with your spirit, the Source part. This connection will allow you to readily attract whatever you want.

<u>Dianne's Initial Feedback</u>

I'm pretty sure I've never been aligned because I rarely feel like a "fountain of well-being," singing Hallelujah and waving my arms back and forth.

Rule 4: Use Your Emotional Radar Detector

What feels good is good because emotions are the message center of the body. The thoughts that make you feel light and breathe easy are the right ones. Move away from anything that feels bad. And pay attention to the warning signs displayed through negative emotions.

<u>Dianne's Initial Feedback</u>

As a strong-minded professional woman, I've been too busy "doing" things to ever acknowledge my emotional center. It's been much easier to ignore exhaustion, sorrow, and frustration than to go into those scary "feeling" places.

Rule 5: Manage Your Wave

Everything has a vibrational flow and we are all connected through energy waves. Create harmony and synergy by focusing on the positive side of the wave.

Dianne's Initial Feedback
It won't be easy to grab at the merry side of the "it's all good" stick. I'll need to redirect my thoughts and look for the small positive things that happened during the day.

Rule 6: Tend to Yourself First

The only person you need to please in life is you. Take 100 percent of the responsibility for your words, actions, and experiences and take care of yourself, first and foremost.

Dianne's Initial Feedback
Abraham tells us to act like a cat. Well, my cat is orange, fat, furry, demanding, and only sits on my lap only when he feels like it. He is, however, quite satisfied with life and always takes care of his needs.

Rule 7: Focus on Receiving

Sit back, remain positive, and let the Universe deliver what you want. Allow yourself to receive.

Dianne's Initial Feedback
I am a professional "earner," so I don't know how to receive without effort and exertion. But it sure would be nice if the Universe just dropped things into my lap.

Rule 8: Choose the Ending to Your Story

Reality is yours to create. Use clear intentions, desires, and positive feelings to manifest whatever you want and watch unlimited futures unfold.

<u>Dianne's Initial Feedback</u>

If my life is a movie in the making, perhaps it will end in love, romance, and travel. Now that sounds pretty exciting.

Rule 9: Manage Your Circle

There are only three "circles" of influence: (1) your circle, (2) other people's circles, and (3) the Universe's circle. Your only job is to manage your circle. Get out of everyone else's business and let them manage themselves.

<u>Dianne's Initial Feedback</u>

Does this mean I'm not responsible for other people and their issues? Can I stop feeling guilty and just let everyone enjoy their day or be miserable, as they have chosen?

Rule 10: Feeling Good Is the Mecca

Lighten up. Move away from resistance and be able to say, "I love how this feels!"

<u>Dianne's Initial Feedback</u>

I mostly feel push-back and strain, but emotional bliss is a terrific future goal.

It's pretty easy to understand Esther Hicks's main concept: Positive thoughts, words, and feelings are the building blocks for a rich, fulfilling life. I got it. Positive ideas lead to positive results. There was only one problem: I had major stinking thinking. My thoughts were hairy and grim, monumentally influenced by generations of Irish and German descendants trained in the art of "disaster talk."

Thinking and speaking optimistically were not part of my standard operating procedures. My parents had wealth and prestige but worried endlessly about my father's career, paying the bills, and every aspect of human life. "Eat all your food. It might be your last meal." "Drive safely! You could get in an accident." "Find a stable job so you can make it through the lean times." "Be careful. It isn't safe to go out at night." And of course, "What will the neighbors think?" This one I never completely understood.

So, I wholeheartedly committed myself to a cleanse, a mental and verbal diet, repeating the mantra, "What you think about, you bring about." I worked on mastering the art of happy talk and painted my world with delightful editorial comments.

I reorganized every utterance before speaking, cutting out negative verbiage. "Have a fabulous trip" instead of "Have a safe trip." I redirected my responses midsentence. "I'm feeling well" rather than "I don't feel good." And I permanently replaced "I'm fine" with "I'm doing great." I even put a rubber band around my wrist and snapped it every time I voiced something undesirable. It took a while, but eventually I stopped bruising my skin and revamped my external delivery.

Along with the flowery commentary, I paid close attention to the joyful events that occurred during the day, no matter how small. I called my observations "The Daily Goodness." Sometimes the goodness was tiny, like having blue skies, narrowly avoiding a parking ticket, or having a non-puffy hair day. Other days, the goodness was great, like winning a raffle prize or receiving a client check in the mail before the due date. Every night at dinner, I instructed the kids, "Tell me at least one good thing that happened to you today." They struggled at first, desperately wanting to discuss their disappointments and frustrations. But with practice, we all became skilled at articulating the good side of the metaphysical stick.

Emma enthusiastically commented, "I got invited to Kristen's birthday party."

"I got an A in spelling," Alexandra chimed.

And I announced, "Someone complimented my hairdo today!"

Over time, I embodied "The Shortcuts," and my external verbal delivery became certifiably stellar. Alas, I still struggled. For some reason, on the inside I was still not humming with everlasting delight.

Just below the surface of my tongue lived a raging critic, an evil She-Devil with long mahogany hair driving a black chariot and cracking a whip, along with her pack of drooling, rabid dogs. This horrible menace screamed loathsome admonitions. *You're fat. You're not organized. You're not smart enough to get the job done. Your clients don't even like you. You don't spend enough time with the kids. You're a terrible mother.* I had fixed my vocabulary with well-crafted sentences, but I was still afraid I couldn't complete my heavy workload, be a good parent, or finish the ever-growing to-do list.

I tried. I really tried to morph my anxiety-filled thoughts into positive bubbles of amber light, but the negative witch remained. While forcing myself to speak of sunshine and rainbows, my clients were demanding, the house a mess, the kids unruly, and the dog and cat endlessly adding to the chaos. To top it off, I found myself feeling sick all day long. Surprise! I was pregnant with my third child.

But I have an entire life to renovate. Instead of becoming a buoyant, joyful woman and an inspiration to all, I morphed into an onerous pregnant inmate. My hormones kicked into high gear, my body became twisted with morning sickness, and my temper flailed into overdrive. Where was my jovial self-talk now?

As the months progressed, every little thing set me off. One day while I was driving the girls to gymnastics, Alexandra, who was nine at the time, saw a bug climbing down the back window next to her head. She grabbed my leather business-card holder and swung at the bug, sailing both the insect and my small case out the window at 45 mph. Her younger sister covered her mouth with both hands in disbelief. Several miles down the road, the child confessed to the crime and I pulled the car over with a screech.

A gush of fury grabbed my gut. It consumed me. Everything went into slow motion as if I were in the middle of a car wreck. Consciousness left my body and I became two people. I heard the She-Devil screaming over my left shoulder, berating my little girl for doing such a thoughtless act to my important card holder. Then an affable fluffy angel appeared, floating above my right shoulder. She assured me in a gentle, syrupy voice, *You can find the business-card holder somewhere in the grass. Why are you screaming?*

The sinister side possessed me as the gruesome devil projected a full-belly roar and gave the sweet angel the finger. I parked the car on the side of the busy median and huffed like a frenzied, snorting bull as I marched my pregnant body and my children back and forth searching for the leather case for over an hour. Eventually, we found it.

The next day, my mother came over to babysit so I could finish an urgent proposal. Instead of playing "house," my daughters chose to play "store." They set up shop in the living room and tried to sell confiscated items like my jewelry, coasters, and the TV remote control to my unsuspecting mother. The prices were high in the fake store, but it was all very innocent.

My mother skipped down the stairs and stuck her head into my damp basement office. "Wow, they want to be little businesswomen just like you," she chimed.

I felt a crack of lightning rake down my spine. I glared at her, my eyes red with rage, and insanely erupted, "Why would anyone want to be like me?"

She looked at me in disbelief. "They love you and want to be like you."

I hurled uncontrollably, "What? They want to be stressed, unhappy, suicidal, and pregnant? No one should have a life as miserable as mine."

This was a bona fide "defining moment." All the merry-talk in the world and pamphlets on Laws of Attraction couldn't soothe the internal skeletons holding me hostage in a cage of self-loathing.

According to another book on my list, *The Biology of Belief*, written by Bruce Lipton, only 20 percent of our life is run by our conscious mind. This is the logical, clear part of the brain responsible for making focused decisions based on reality and results. The remaining 80 percent of our brain is navigated by our unconscious mind, our child brain. This part is primitive, reactionary, and totally irrational.

When it comes to sheer neurological processing abilities, the subconscious mind is millions of times more powerful than the conscious mind. If the desires of the conscious mind conflict with the programs of the subconscious mind, which "mind" do you think will win out? You can repeat the positive affirmation that you are lovable over and over or that your cancer tumor will shrink. But if, as a child you heard . . . that you are worthless and sickly, those messages programmed in your subconscious mind will undermine your best conscious efforts to change your life.

—Bruce Lipton, Ph.D., *The Biology of Belief*

Our child brain is the crazy bus driver who careens madly down the middle of the road when a "hot button" gets pushed. The unconscious mind is programmed from youth and knows fight or flight, pleasure or pain, based on early childhood experiences with joy, drama, or trauma. Every wounding, painful experience in childhood becomes a pattern that influences who we become as an adult.

My childhood was quite distressing. In active pursuit of my father's financial career, our family moved from state to state as he climbed the corporate ladder. Due to the timing of each move, I changed schools every three years and found it nearly impossible to develop long-term attachments to friends, teachers, or schoolmates.

My family dynamics were also less than ideal. My mother was passive and fearful and my father was an aggressive, driven, intellectual man who ruled with an iron fist. In our household, there was no tolerance for complaints or openness to personal expression: "Stop crying or I'll give you something to cry about!" "Follow the rules or wait until your father gets home!" None of us kids were dumb enough to grossly misbehave and experience the fury or the belt attached to the imposing threats.

As I aged, the unresolved issues from my past festered and ballooned out of control, especially those of abandonment and lack of self-worth. I kept moving faster toward society's highly publicized goals: own a business, make lots of money, get married, raise a family in suburbia, sign kids up for a million activities, and always be the perfect mom with a peppermint-colored lipstick smile. I followed the formula but my inner child was dying, heaped in a moldy pile of goo. I had a crusty layer of wounds that were old, brown, and smelly. Without releasing the buried anguish from youth, I couldn't get my soul stream back into the flow.

I didn't want to bring a new baby into my home as a deranged, depressed woman. I needed a professional cleanup crew to properly recondition my mind. Right then and there, I called the Hoffman Institute and signed up for eight days of emotional rehab.

⨳ 3 ⨳

Course Correction

"I will rediscover my passion, leaving nothing repressed or undone. I will re-create myself: lose weight, perform in the theater, improve my relationship, journal my stories, and find a career to help others grow. I will fulfill these dreams!"

∿

In blind faith, I attended the Hoffman Institute. I entered the program a little girl walking down a murky lane, legs covered in the black vines of self-judgment and loathing. Over the course of a week, I committed my energy toward healing and explicitly followed their instructions. I reviewed the details regarding how my childhood had shaped my current adult life. I was the by-product of both my mother's and father's imprinting. Part of me had become an angry, rage-aholic work slave like my father, serving the company first, and another part of me had become a vacuous mother, desolate and over-whelmed by caring for everyone else's needs but never my own. I had followed a "traditional" course but the results were abhorrently unsatisfying.

What I didn't know at the time, was that I had chosen the perfect place to work out my issues. More than seventy thousand people in twelve countries have attended this highly acclaimed emotional self-recovery mecca since its inception in 1967, including celebrity graduates such as Grammy winners Kenny Logins, Bonnie Raitt, Bill Medley, and Roseanne Cash. Plus, Hoffman has conducted an ongoing leadership program at Harvard University documenting its success in producing long-term positive emotional change.

> The Harvard University peer research shows that the Hoffman Process participants experienced reductions in depression, anxiety, and obsessive/compulsive tendencies, coupled with lasting significant increase in emotional intelligence, life satisfaction, compassion, vitality, and forgiveness.
>
> —*Explore: The Journal of Science and Healing,*
> November/December 2006

I can't fully explain what happened to me at Hoffman's weeklong spiritual boot camp. And like all Hoffman graduates, I must honor the confidentiality agreement I signed promising not to disclose personal stories from the Process. But what I can say is that on the first day, I sat in a circle in a beautiful retreat house in Napa Valley, where I'd spend a lot of time that week, and looked around the room, sizing up the strangers seated next to me. I saw a troubled woman with an oversized shawl wrapped tightly around her head and shoulders; an uptight, buttoned-up businesswoman; an attention-seeking actor from the Valley; an ingénue in her twenties; and a tough-guy shipbuilder from New England. I wanted to jump up and run out the door. *What was I doing here? I have nothing in common with these people.*

But I would soon learn that I was dead wrong. I had everything in common with these searching souls. We had all been imprinted with both the positive and negative qualities we'd observed from our parents. According to Bob Hoffman, "All children want love and attention from their parents. Children believe implicitly that Mom and Dad make correct decisions and know what they're doing at all times. For a child, imitating a parent's behaviors, moods, and attitudes—literally becoming like them—often seems the only way to earn a parent's love and attention. When a child takes on his or her parents' negativities in an attempt to be loveable to the parents, he or she becomes a victim of the Negative Love Syndrome."

Using a complex mix of profound techniques including visualization, meditation, cathartic journaling, Gestalt, group therapy, and some Eastern mysticism, the process boiled down for me a lifetime of "therapy" into just eight days and "surgically" removed my unwanted negative patterns.

In just a week, I was able to excavate my bruised and tattered psyche and found genuine transformational healing. I bared my soul and discovered a lustrous, resplendent being. I finally saw the real "me" in full glory as a smart, creative woman who loved to dance, sing, and perform. I was both an artist and an intellectual. I removed the fears, chains, and self-hatred and flew back to Chicago with my head held high.

Standing in O'Hare Airport, I watched my two joyful children run toward me. My heart was bursting open. I had a new glowing love for these remarkable kids and for myself. I fell to my knees next to the baggage carousel and sat on the airport floor with a Gandhi-like grin, pregnant, embracing two little girls with my husband beside me. I experienced compassion for all Earthly creatures.

In that moment, I committed to "living in the long run." I would awaken all the possibilities for my life and take chances. I quietly repeated the promise I'd made during the Hoffman retreat. "I will live as my authentic self with no excuses or apologies. I will rediscover my passion, leaving nothing repressed or undone. I will re-create myself: lose weight, perform in the theater, improve my relationship, journal my stories, and find a career to help others grow. I will fulfill these dreams!" These were not just affirmations. Somehow, I was going to make it happen.

Miraculously, the Hoffman process also left me with a mental Ty-D-Bol wash. When I got home, the depression had lifted. I was no longer the gallant queen of sadness. The steamer trunk of internal damage was empty and I could look in the mirror with long-overdue acknowledgment and respect: "I'm a good mother. I'm a hard worker. I'm clever and capable, and gosh darn it, people like me."

A warmhearted glow radiated from the inside. I wasn't Snow White, whistling cheerful tunes all day, but nice thoughts and words flowed readily. The internal She-Devil remained quiet. I stood strong, capable, and worthy of respect. Over and over again I repeated a highly relevant quote I found by Rita Davenport: "If money can fix it, it's not a problem."

I no longer fretted or twirled about the small stuff. Little things didn't bother me. Spilled milk, toys strewn across the floor, misplaced keys, coffee stains on my blouse, traffic jams, and fender benders left me with an emotional flat line, and fortunately this time, my pleasant disposition wasn't chemically induced by Prozac.

One day, when I arrived home from a trip to the grocery store, Rob announced that Emma had kicked off her shoe and crashed it into my antique Victorian chocolate pot. It was my favorite gift, an intricately hand-painted burgundy pottery that now lay broken on the floor in a million pieces. I called Emma over for a chat. "You're responsible for your actions. You kicked your shoe off and broke Mommy's favorite present. It wasn't yours; it was mine. You need to make it right and find a way to replace the damaged item. You'll have to save up your money and together we'll replace it." *Who is this sane woman?* She was so reasonable and sound. I didn't recognize her.

My calm, rational demeanor continued as the weeks passed. With the holidays around the corner, I took my ten-foot-long living room rug in for a professional carpet cleaning. A week later, I brought it home and dragged it across the floor, using my pregnant belly as a shelf. Struggling, I put the furniture back and checked the task off my list.

Shortly afterward, our insane Wheaten terrier trotted into the living room, lifted his leg, and urinated down the side of my velvet couch, leaving a large circular puddle on the freshly cleaned rug. Much to my credit, I didn't fly off the handle. I just grimaced and asked the kids to help me move the smelly thing back into the car for a second round of sanitization.

Over the next couple of months, my relationship with the girls dramatically improved and I was thrilled to learn I'd soon be having a baby boy. Unhappily, my marital connection was still weak. Occasionally, Rob would lean over the banister on his way up to bed and squeak, "What are you doing?" From the basement I'd respond, "I am working till late." He'd just mutter, "Alright." And that was about it. Rob agreed to attend the Hoffman Institute after the baby was born and I reminded myself, "If I can continue to grow and appreciate myself on the inside, perhaps I can find my way back into love on the outside." Anything's possible.

My first two children were delivered naturally and I expected nothing different from the third. I couldn't have been more surprised when after eight hours of arduous, painful spasms and body contortions, my uterus stopped contracting.

The doctor waltzed in and claimed, "You have a lazy uterus!" He swung around and alerted the nurses' station, "Prepare for an emergency C-section."

"No!" I screamed from flat on my back, a mountainous stomach sticking up in the air. "This isn't what I had planned." In exchange for a signature on the surgery papers, the doctor promised to give me a tubal ligation and I agreed to the deal. They wheeled me into the operating room and one hour later I held my healthy seven-pound baby, Adam.

I spent the next couple of days in the hospital recuperating with Adam by my side. Unfortunately, the pregnancy, in combination with lousy Irish genes, created a new medical issue. Normally, Cesarean patients complain about the hip-to-hip staples, but I was howling in pain about my right calf, which throbbed with heated varicosity. Just like in *Night of the Living Dead*, gross, ropy, wormlike veins protruded from my thigh to ankle. As soon as we got home, I scheduled an appointment to see a vein specialist.

I entered the exam room and an aged, ornery doctor tottered behind me. He wore a starched lab coat and had long bushy gray eyebrows that stood straight out from his head. The man clicked his tongue as he poked at my bare leg. His brown eyes dashed back and forth and then he gruffly announced, "You need surgery to strip the veins from your ankle to your hip, immediately."

"I just had a C-section," I replied. "I'm not ready for more surgery."

He ignored me. "Young lady, these veins need to come out right now, or it could lead to a serious blood clot or stroke. I'd be very worried about you if you were my daughter."

I shot back in response, "I'm not your daughter and I can't sign up for cuts to my body. I need to start my new life."

The surgeon continued, emotionless. "In nonmedical terms, the veins are permanently stripped after carrying the weight of three babies. You have a deep venous disorder and will probably need twenty-pound compression stockings even after the surgery!"

I gasped, "I have to wear grandma support hose for the rest of my life?" This horrid man had just signed my fashion death warrant. *Doesn't he know I'm forty, not eighty?* Forget the health implications and two required surgeries. *I can't wear skirts anymore. I'll be a freak all summer strutting around in shorts and supp-hose looking like the Saturday Night Live Church Lady! I don't want to be a pantsuit maven.* Money definitely couldn't fix this problem. I sank down to the floor right there in front of the mean doctor, mortified.

For a week, I fretted and fussed about my infirmity but finally, an epiphany emerged. This was an opportunity in disguise. If I could accept "what is," or as I affectionately call the "is-ness" and walk around with a freakish calf-wrap, I could teach my kids a crucial life lesson: We must love our uniquely imperfect bodies. We need to embrace the good and the not-so-good without feeling self-conscious or embarrassed. It's about accepting the pimples, high arches, frizzy hair, allergies, cold sores, and blue veins with our head held high.

From now on, when anyone points to a scar or bruise, I'll just pull up my pants and show them my lifelong ecru companion, a sumptuous stocking. I quickly accepted my fate and scheduled the two sequential vein surgeries. Somehow this malady activated my sense of determination and I knew: *It was time to come of age, middle age, that is.* I liked the real me, inside and out, and nothing was going to stand in my way.

Thus, I began my personal renewal process by "whiteboarding" myself. I took out a large dry-erase board and a box of colorful markers and wrote down the answers to the following questions: Who do you want to be as a woman? Who do you want to be as a partner? Who do you want to be as a parent? Who do you want to be as yourself? What do you want your life to look like? What do you love to do, see, hear, and feel?

I answered each question and made a comprehensive "I Love It" inventory, prioritizing the list from the heart. Acting, theater, dance, and singing were on the top, along with horseback riding, ice skating, hiking, travel, and adventure.

~

SECTION II

Body and Soul Reboot

~

4

"All the World's a Stage . . ."

Nerves hijacked my body and my hands started shaking uncontrollably. I wrapped them tightly behind my back and proceeded to squeak out sixteen pitchy bars of "Wouldn't It Be Loverly?" My singing was so bad I wanted to keel over and die right then and there in the musical audition. It would have been fitting for the occasion.

≈

E ven though I'd acted in both high school and college, it had been nearly twenty years since I had stepped on a stage. I'd shut performing arts out of my life when my father bellowed, "Acting is a shit career. You'll never be able to support yourself and I won't support you." He commanded, "Be a nurse or a doctor!" As a dutiful daughter, I put my ardent desire for a theatrical degree on the back burner and pursued nursing at Marquette University instead. There, I discovered that I couldn't stand the smell of urine or the sight of blood. I quickly dropped out of the acclaimed nursing program and chose psychology and philosophy instead, for lack of any better idea at the time. But now I needed to openly embrace my passion and find a way back on to the stage.

The She-Devil awoke from her slumber and jeered, *Actors are beautiful and thin. They have perfect faces and bodies. You are too fat to get into acting. No one will give you a role when you're so out of shape.*

In truth, I'd been fighting the battle of the bulge my whole life, and after delivering Adam, I was at an all-time high of one hundred eighty pounds. A roll of lard hung over the top of my pants, jiggling like a fresh bowl of Jell-O, and my cellulite-ridden saddlebag quaked with every step. To make matters worse, although the surgeries had successfully removed miles of broken pipes, my legs were still red, bruised, and swollen.

In true Scarlett O'Hara fashion, I refused to give in. "As God is my witness, I'll never surrender!" I put my fingers in my ears and hummed a tune to mute the She-Devil. *I won't listen to any more anti-acting mental messages. I'll lace up my fat with a tight girdle, wear a loose skirt, and zip up some tall boots to hide the support hose. I will audition my little heart out!*

Based on "The Shortcuts," I knew it was important to have clear goals, so I addressed the following strategic question: *What specifically do you want to achieve in the theater?* A mental image popped into my mind's eye: I was on a dark wooden stage in a chorus line, wearing petticoats, dancing the cancan, and smiling from ear to ear. I felt the heat from the canned lights and heard the audience roar. I drew the image on a piece of paper, a ridiculous stick girl on a stage in an outrageous lace corset and long puffy dress, mouth open wide, wildly kicking pencil legs in the air. The picture made me laugh. I clearly stated my intention. "I want to sing and dance in a local musical production."

Musical talent is obviously a critical requirement. So in an attempt to shape up my rusty, flat voice, I pulled out an old songbook from the piano bench and worked every day plunking out a tune from the theatrical show My Fair Lady. Now, I just needed an opportunity to shine.

The following week, while dropping Emma off at day-care, I'm not sure exactly why, but I randomly mentioned my creative interests to her preschool teacher. The young woman turned around and gestured toward the door. She stated, "The woman who just walked into the hallway is a community theater veteran. She can tell you every-thing you need to know about performing arts in this area." This was the first of many Brass Ring Moments that would guide me through my renovation. It was as if a Divine force had dropped a glowing silver arrow into the room and pointed me out the door.

I barreled into the corridor and cornered the unsus-pecting stranger by her child's locker. I introduced myself and expressed my desire to get involved with local musical theater. She smiled pleasantly and graciously shared with me everything she knew about the League of North Shore Theatres. I listened intently and took notes. I thanked her profusely and, as instructed, rushed out to buy a local newspaper so I could search for upcoming auditions.

There it was, the ideal opportunity. In just two weeks, the Glencoe Community Theatre would be holding audi-tions for Oliver! on my birthday. Awesome things always seemed to happen on my birthday.

On audition day, it took me two hours to artfully apply makeup and craft an outfit to mask my jostling body. I entered the community center and found the room bus-tling with other apprehensive adults. I nervously paced back and forth in a corner; my heart was racing. Eventu-ally, I was escorted into a sparsely appointed classroom with a friendly pianist perched behind the piano, and on the far side of a folding table sat a grimacing director, a bored producer, and an energetic choreographer.

I walked in, gave the director my application, and handed my sheet music to the smiling face behind the upright. The pianist tapped out the song introduction with fervor. Nerves hijacked my body and my hands started shaking uncontrollably. I wrapped them tightly behind my back and proceeded to squeak out sixteen pitchy bars of "Wouldn't It Be Loverly?" My singing was so bad I wanted to keel over and die right then and there in the musical audition. It would have been fitting for the occasion.

The dramatic team behind the table politely nodded, "Thank you." And I seized this moment to offer an explanation.

I implored, "I'm very sorry. I've been on a long acting hiatus and my vocal chords are terribly tight. I will sound much better with a bit of practice, but I just *have* to get back into the theater and perform!" Suddenly, the director shot up and handed me a two-page script and asked me to read for the part of Nancy, the female lead. My nerves tingled as I copped a pose and slipped into a guttural Cockney accent. The acting part was much easier than butchering a musical number with shrill pipes. The woman smiled and appeared pleased as she escorted me to the door.

I ran all the way to the parking lot shaking from head to toe, screaming, "Ahhhhhhh!" I jumped up and down in the snow to move the massive adrenaline that was coursing throughout my body. I was proud of myself for taking such a huge step. I got inside the car and loudly cheered, " Congratulations! What chutzpah. What guts."

My audition had been terrible, but the important thing was that I had shown up. Now, all I had to do was wait.

The director called the next day and offered me the role of Townsperson One. It was a miracle! I had two lines and would be wearing a red corset and petticoats. How about that! I had officially made it into the chorus. Better yet, I had achieved a major life goal. I was now an actor. I strutted around beaming for days.

I knew I had to polish up my theatrical skills, so I found a professional acting studio in Chicago and registered for adult scene-study classes. I also researched the city's best master vocal coach and begged her to fix my dreadful voice. She took pity on me and let me enroll.

5

Battle of the Bulge

*I ate to suppress the sadness and solitude that had con-
sumed my early years. As a budding teenager, I tried every
one of the weight-loss clubs. I was a member of Weight-
Watchers, Jenny Craig, Nutrisystem, and yes, Overeaters
Anonymous. "Hi, I am Dianne and I am an overeater."
That's right.*

~

I had three months of rehearsal before opening night and
it was imperative that I get serious about my weight. I
was born pleasingly plump and stayed that way throughout childhood as we moved across the States. My mother
gave birth to me in an army hospital in Virginia and after
my father finished his military term two years later, we
moved to the south side of Chicago so he could begin his
financial career. When I was in kindergarten, we moved
to the suburbs in northern Illinois and then to Arizona
for third and fourth grade. Finally, we settled into Indiana
for the middle school years.

Very early on, my survival mechanism for coping
with upheaval was hoarding food. I kept my bedroom

booby-trapped with snacks, treats, and desserts strategically hidden in the sock drawer, my pink cowboy boots, and on the slats underneath my bed. Throughout the day I sought comfort from my friends, Ding Dong and Suzy Q, and at night I sucked on Caramel Cream Bulls-Eyes and Mary Janes. I was such a skilled professional, my mother never found the stash.

I vividly remember going to the doctor's office in seventh grade. The forceful nurse demanded that I step on the gunmetal gray scale in the middle of a busy hallway. I was only five foot three and the weights tipped at one hundred fifty pounds. I literally fell off backward in shock. As I got older, I got taller and wider. Excess weight became the albatross around my neck. I entered high school in Indianapolis blossoming at one hundred sixty pounds on a five-foot-six frame.

In freshman year, one picturesque spring day I walked home and took a moment to squat down and admire the pacific bluebells emerging from the soil. There, I heard it: the voice of a malicious neighbor child bellowing from behind the protection of a nearby boxwood hedge. "Hey there, Thunder Thighs! I can see your thighs shake when you walk!" I felt the beast's words like a glass dagger stab into my chest cavity, piercing through the organs. I spun around, humiliated, trying to get a glimpse of the assailant, but he remained hidden. I thundered all the way to my front door. The accuracy of the boy's comment made the agonizing wound even more excruciating.

I decided to take action. I looked through my mom's collection of *Good Housekeeping* magazines and found the magic cure. There it was . . . the grapefruit-and-egg-white diet. I took a solemn oath to follow the formula, eating nothing but grapefruit, egg whites, and lettuce every day for two months. Hunger pangs became my red badge of courage. I started exercising, doing jumping jacks, and speed walking around the block. By the beginning of my sophomore year, I had dropped down to my champion weight of one hundred thirty-seven pounds. For the first time since birth, I was light, fit, and radiant.

I was so confident, I tried out for the cheerleading squad and made it! Actually, there wasn't much competition, but that wasn't the point. Another staggering event took place. Chris, the captain of our high school football team, invited me to the homecoming dance. He wasn't the brightest boy in the school, but he was cute and had adorable dimples. More importantly, he was popular. Today we might label him as a "tool," but I had a prime date to the dance and, as a bonus, I was momentarily popular. So, off I went on my first date to homecoming, dancing to "Stayin' Alive" and drinking Hawaiian Punch all night. Chris's dad waited in the car as this adorable young stud walked me to my front door. He paused for a moment and moved in for what would have been my first good-night peck. In fear, I turned my cheek. This is a missed opportunity I will always regret.

At sixteen, my life was fabulous. I had a cute figure, cheerleader status, straight A's, and a theatrical role as a dancer in the hit school musical, *Kiss Me, Kate*. This was the first time in my life I'd ever felt "deliriously happy." That's when it happened again: My father announced that we were moving, this time from Indianapolis to Chicago. That was the day the planet stopped revolving. Everything I'd worked so hard to create was permanently destroyed in that moment.

And just like any respectable steer lining up for slaughter, I mooed, wailed, and ate my way from a size six back up to a size eighteen in a matter of months. I ballooned to one hundred seventy pounds and walked in as the new fat girl dressed in a plaid uniform skirt at a mean, estrogen-filled Catholic all-female high school in Illinois. It was a living teenage hell.

I decided to keep myself busy and found a weekend sales position at Marshall Field's, a local retailer. The human resources professional assigned me to the fine chocolates department. Can you believe it? I was surrounded by boxes of my best friend and faithful companion, succulent sweets.

After working on the job for a few weeks, a well-dressed gentleman in his twenties walked in, apparently looking for a gift. The man approached the counter with an eerie grin and queried me directly, "What are the best chocolates in the case?" As an expert in the subject, I joyfully pointed my thick index finger at the French truffles, raspberry creams, and Frango mints. After all, it was my job to be knowledgeable. "Now I can see why you are so fat!" he matter-of-factly exclaimed.

I felt my face burn crimson as the familiar knife blade hit my solar plexus. It's one thing to look in the mirror and think you're disgusting and fat, and something completely different to have it confirmed by a complete stranger, twice. I stumbled backward into the tiny stockroom and closed the organ-fold door. I sat down, huddled on the floor for what seemed like hours, until Beelzebub eventually left the candy section empty-handed.

Soon thereafter, I requested a transfer to the men's clothing department and I acknowledged my acute eating disorder: I ate to suppress the sadness and solitude that had consumed my early years. As a budding teenager, I tried every one of the weight-loss clubs. I was a member of WeightWatchers, Jenny Craig, Nutrisystem, and yes,

Overeaters Anonymous. "Hi, I am Dianne and I am an overeater." That's right. But it didn't matter because all the books, tapes, pep talks, programs, and clubs couldn't fix my obsession.

Decades later at my *Oliver!* audition, I weighed as much as a heavyweight prizefighter, but somehow I felt different; I felt whole. I had finished Hoffman, delivered my third child, and landed a chorus role. I was stupendously proud of myself and ready to be the person I came here to be. I refused to let fat rule my world. I desperately wanted to meet the version of me who was not encased in flab. I stated my second goal out loud, "I want to be the weight of a healthy five-foot-six woman, around one hundred forty pounds."

I kicked off my pre-play weight-loss expedition by reading Geneen Roth's book *When Food Is Love*. Her phenomenal advice resonated with everything I'd already learned about self-awareness and honoring our experiences within.

> Diets and food plans enable adults to remain children, victims of oppressive familial and cultural systems in which they spend their lives punishing themselves for not being good enough . . . The real reasons (they feel they can't eat what they want) are that if they begin to be kind to themselves around food, if they actually let themselves have what they want and do not punish themselves afterward, then their fathers, mothers, their teachers, their lovers, everyone who treated them with mistrust, anyone by whom they were violated or abused, everyone about whom they have an

investment in not recognizing the truth, will have been wrong. In discovering that they are worth being kind to, worth living with compassion and abundance, they unfold softly into a journey of self-discovery that changes their lives forever.

—Geneen Roth, *When Food Is Love*

Roth recommends that we listen to our own guidance system and let our body guide us back to a healthy weight. I absorbed her suggestions and started paying attention to my natural signals.

Even though I'd abused my body with food for forty years, there had to be a Hungry/Full meter somewhere inside. Hopefully, it wasn't permanently broken. I simply had to find the on/off switch, the one that told me when to eat and when to shut down, satisfied but not overly full. I began by charting my stomach's normal cycles and found several trends: I am typically hungry at ten in the morning and three in the afternoon; I move from feeling full to ravenous in a matter of seconds, often without warning; and I fill up very quick after consuming small servings of food.

Armed with this information, I came up with the Dianne Diet Plan, a totally creative portion-reduction program comprising three major components: The Full Meter, The Clock, and The Leftovers. It was a feast-and-famine regimen. Roth said I could eat whatever I wanted, so during daylight hours I consumed small portions of hamburgers, French fries, and even a dripping cheesy Reuben with sauerkraut. Then, I waited for the "full feeling" to really kick in. At 5:00 p.m., I cut myself off from all highly indulgent food, hypothetically locking the fridge until the next morning. This was the famine part. If I was starving at night, I'd steam vegetables, eat a bowl of fruit, or sip a cup of hot tea. As part of this unconventional diet, I also allowed myself to indulge in a piece of decadently rich chocolate every day. These simple rituals became a winning formula.

I also came to terms with my acute chewing disorder. Somehow, I must have gotten stuck in the oral phase as a child, because I "needed" to chew to process stress and focus my attention. In fact, I chewed so often and hard, I'm sure my jaw was the strongest muscle in my body. Here's the encouraging news: Chewing is not the same as eating. Instead of consuming mass quantities of food, I used the white minty goodness of Chiclets to satisfy my nerves. This allowed me to flap my jaws and not add any significant calories to the hips. I danced, sang on stage, and ate during the daylight hours. Triumphantly, the weight fell off and by opening night, I'd dropped forty pounds.

I've remained the same weight for twelve years by eating small portions of whatever food I wanted and by weighing myself every day to monitor the progress, or hopefully, lack thereof. I openly admit to an arduous battle with two pounds that somehow maliciously attach themselves to my muffin top every month. It's especially hard during the harsh winter shut-in period in the Midwest, but I just go back on the plan and remove the annoying weight over and over again.

Truthfully, my brain is still obsessed with thoughts of food, but I'm proud of my ability to wrestle this major life addiction to the ground. Someday I'd like to have a tiny, skinny bikini body like Demi Moore, but perhaps I'll set that goal for myself in my senior years.

～

SECTION III

Manifestation Made Easy

～

≈ 6 ≈

The American Dream

I'd always wanted to live across from the lake, drive a red convertible, and wear clingy designer suits to important business meetings. Now it was my turn! The economy was strong and I knew I had the experience, references, and pedigree to create my own version of the American Dream.

∼

Two years had passed since my fateful psychic meeting and now I had a mind full of positive thoughts, a baby boy, and a new body, and I gleefully landed a supporting role as Sister Sophia in a community theater production of *The Sound of Music*. My internal world was sound and stable and I could finally return my attention to the art of manifestation.

Nassim Haramein is a modern physicist known for his unified field theory, "The Power of Spin," in which he presents groundbreaking evidence proving we are all part of one cosmic source. His popular DVD titled *Black Whole* also offers a coherent model for the structure of the space-time continuum in which the Universe is identified as a "self-organizing vacuum."

According to Haramein, if an individual is aware of themselves and their relationships, they can feed information in the form of thought energy into the "vacuum," or "space" as we know it. These thoughts will then be manifested into physical form. Haramein calls this effect "synchronicity." He also notes that since others are inputting their desires into the system at the same time, the final outcome may be slightly morphed or modified from our original request.

I witnessed the miracle of synchronicity when I clearly wrote down my desire to become part of the theater world. The Universe matched my vision with a singing, dancing chorus-line role and a fluffy petticoat-lined costume. Now I was ready to test Haramein's mental manifestation playground by experimenting with the vacuum deliberately. I wanted to see if I could become a mental Houdini, attracting highly specific items to myself using thought alone.

I crafted a short list of my initial desires: *I want gourmet chocolates, the perfect parking space, and comfortable yet fashionable designer shoes.*

I'm extremely fussy about chocolate and like only the European supremely rich kind. I began my first metaphysical experiment by placing a mental order for a box of Belgian delicacies. I looked up toward the heavens and requested loudly, "I want a box of Godiva chocolates, please." I reviewed the scrumptious flavors in my mind: Midnight Swirl, Almond Praline, and Caramel Embrace. I imagined the bittersweet pool of smooth lusciousness as it melted on my tongue. I cut out a picture from a magazine featuring a bonbon as a visual reminder, and of course, I flatly refused to buy a single morsel for myself. After all, this was manifestation practice. The treats had to come to me.

After placing my virtual order, I promptly returned to everyday life, not knowing how long the experiment would take. Approximately two weeks later, the FedEx man rang my doorbell in the middle of a busy business day. I ran up from the basement and signed for a medium-sized shipping box from an investment banking firm. I closed the door and inquisitively unwrapped the package, discovering a large assortment of Godiva. "Chocolates for me?" I cooed. I examined the box, searching for a note. Oh, no! The box was addressed to a woman named Dianna Devine. "Wow, what a huge disappointment. The candy isn't for me!" I whined.

Incredibly disheartened, I ran to the phone and called the investment company listed on the shipping label. I explained the error and let the receptionist know I had not yet opened the beloved sweets. Her voice kindly replied, "Thank you for calling. Ms. Devine used to live at your address. We will find her new location and send her another box. Enjoy your chocolates." I cheered for my victory.

I let one Godiva melt in my mouth every day for the next two weeks. Then I got a little cocky. *If I can do this once, I can do it again, but this time I want another brand: Fannie May.* Using the same process, I focused on the objects of my desire, Fruit Fudge, Trinidads, and Mint Meltaways. I stated my new request to the cosmos. "I would like an assortment of Fannie May chocolate candies delivered to me."

A few weeks later, an old friend from college stopped by our house for a visit. She walked straight into the kitchen and handed me a Colonial Assortment of Fannie May candy. I sprang to my feet and applauded wildly, "These are my favorite!" I graciously accepted the fattening box and strutted around feeling like a chocolate-manifestation guru.

After such success, I turned my focus to one of the city's most desirable acquisitions: metered parking. You might think finding a parking spot is simple, but in Chicago, it's a precious commodity. Two hours in a garage could cost up to forty dollars, but a meter, less than five dollars. Needless to say, competition is fierce. People hunt aggressively for emerging spots by blocking traffic, flashing hazard lights, and driving backward down streets. Chocolates make me smile, but parking stresses me out.

My weekly acting class was located in the Loop, so at the beginning of each trip, I looked up and insisted, "Please, Universe, grant me a parking space within one block of the acting studio." As I entered the freeway ramp, I reached inside for a feeling of confidence and tried to imagine myself parallel parking into the perfect spot. Unfortunately, based on my experience, I had one giant problem. I had doubt, and lots of it. I didn't trust the Universe's ability to deliver. When I got downtown, I circled one, two, three city blocks, watching other people grab spaces right in front of me. Late and frustrated, I swung into an obscenely priced garage, cursing under my breath. This happened three weeks in a row.

By the fourth week, I gave up hope. I accepted my unlucky fate and drove down the highway, focusing on the acting script that was not yet memorized for class. Right when I pulled up in front of the arts building, there it was: a perfect rock-star parking space. I screamed with delight and did a victory dance in the driver's seat. It may have been luck, fate, or even deliberate manifestation, but to me it represented mind-over-matter success. Somehow, when I'd released the urgency and sailed downtown feeling relaxed and secure, my luck changed. For the next month, I intuitively found easily accessible metered spots every time.

From that day forward, manifestation became an exciting game of Synchronicity Bingo: request and delivery. Every product that I wanted miraculously popped into view. I stumbled upon a hard-to-find hair conditioner in the window of a beauty salon next to my dentist's office. Bingo. I found the perfect pair of comfortable yet pointy Stuart Weitzman patent pumps in a discount boutique. Bingo. And when I asked the Universe for a new Mileage Plus credit card with double miles, an application appeared in my mailbox the next day. Okay, maybe the credit-card application was just excellent bulk-mail timing, but it was exactly what I'd requested. Bingo. Eventually, finding and receiving items became effortless.

It was early 2003 and things were running smoothly. I felt powerful, so much so that I upgraded my manifestation experiments to a whole new level.

We were living in the North Shore at the time, surrounded by palatial homes, and our house looked like the one owned by the Little Old Lady Who Lived in a Shoe. We had packed two adults and three children into a miniscule 1902 farmhouse and spent time together in one large room that conveniently played the roles of living, dining, and family room combined. Our house was crammed with furniture, electronics, and baby gear. I had to put my office in the unfinished basement, a pressboard desk carefully balanced on cinder blocks in between two trails of groundwater seepage because there simply was no other space in the house. Meanwhile, our neighbors paraded around in fancy cars and carried Louis Vuitton bags. They belonged to country clubs, had live-in nannies, and skied in Vail during winter break. *Why did they have so much and we had so little?*

I'd always wanted to live across from the lake, drive a red convertible, and wear clingy designer suits to important business meetings. Now it was my turn! The economy was strong and I knew I had the experience, references, and pedigree to create my own version of the American Dream. Well, that's what America is all about anyway, manifesting stuff . . . right?

I stood tall and spread my arms wide and asked the Universe to send me exactly what I wanted: two hundred thousand dollars of new marketing contracts. I needed big clients who managed even bigger budgets. I knew I'd have to buckle down, work long hours, and significantly boost my bank account. I focused my mind, body, and energy on the sales process and remembered the sense of exhilaration that surrounds a large corporate contact.

Much to my surprise, business projects marched right in. Within a month, a new client asked me to bid on a rebranding program, a past client reengaged their marketing plan, and a business associate handed me a sizable marketing campaign. Suddenly I had three deals that, when completed, would meet my financial goal.

For the next year, I climbed aboard the work-till-you-drop train. I woke up at 6:30 a.m., got the kids ready, and took them to school. During the day, I ran around like a madwoman, attending meetings and hastily conducting marketing research from my damp home office. When it was time for the school bell to ring, I jumped in my old green station wagon and chauffeured the kids around to piano lessons and Gymboree, dumping something edible on the table for dinner. As soon as Rob walked in the door, I threw the children at him and ran back into the basement to work. Five-hour energy drinks, Starbucks-stained reports, and midnight client emails were all part of my routine. I was exhausted but earned enough cash to upgrade the wagon to a red-hot Saab '93 convertible. And we'd been approved for a $965,000 super-jumbo loan. My dream was about to become reality.

I also became inspired by a quote in Jack Canfield's book *The Success Principles*.

When Olympic decathlon gold medalist Bruce Jenner asked a roomful of Olympic hopefuls if they had a list of written goals, every one raised their hands. When he asked how many of them had that list with them right that moment, only one person raised their hand. That person was Dan O'Brien. And it was Dan O'Brien who went on to win the gold medal in the decathlon at the 1996 Olympics in Atlanta. Don't underestimate the power of setting goals and constantly reviewing them.

—Jack Canfield, *The Success Principles*

In earnest, I absorbed Canfield's message and carefully made a list of requirements for my future residence. I called the list my "I Wants:" I want a large, ready-made Georgian, Colonial, or Victorian home within walking distance of Lake Michigan with five bedrooms, an office, two-car garage, sunroom, and a finished attic and basement. I didn't care about a fancy kitchen or big yard, so I kept those items off the list. I printed up a tiny version and taped it on the front page of my Day-Timer so it could serve as a periodic reminder of my desires.

Housing prices in our area were high; a decent home started at eight hundred thousand dollars, and lakeside mansions were running three million. Every day, I perused the Internet for listings and talked to my realtor, Beth. For months, I dragged the family around to open houses, but none of the residences in our price range came close to meeting the extensive requirements.

Finally, I stumbled upon a three-story Victorian palace with intricate baby blue trim. It was a stunning five-bedroom masterpiece with vaulted ceilings, an expansive third-floor office, and a fully renovated kitchen. The house was not near the lake and was priced at $1.1 million, but I was exhausted from the endless house-hunting grind and wanted it to be over.

Impulsively, Rob and I took the plunge and tossed out a low-ball bid for the turn-of-the-century chateau. I felt a sting inside my torso and my hand jerked as I signed the paperwork for more money than we could afford. Later that day, another couple threw down a more sizable bid and we lost the Victorian beauty. At first, I was devastated, but my feelings quickly morphed into relief when I realized we'd been foolish to over-commit and were tremendously lucky to walk away unscathed.

What really concerned me, however, was the fact that the manifestation process wasn't working. I'd been looking at my "I Want" list every day, investing all my time into the house-hunting process and remaining positive. *So where was my darn house? What was I doing wrong? Didn't I deserve a nice place to live?*

Disappointed and mentally fried, I decided to fly the family to Fort Lauderdale for a long-overdue spring vacation. We arrived at the hotel, immediately pulled on our bathing suits, and raced down to the sun-drenched Atlantic. Right there at the water's edge, my cell phone rang. It was Beth. "Dianne, you've got to see the new house that was just listed on the market today. It has unobstructed views of Lake Michigan, five bedrooms, a four-season porch with French doors that could serve as an office, a two-car attached garage, and it's in your price range."

My heart sank into the sand beneath me. I screamed, "Are you kidding? Is this a joke? You're telling me 'my house' materialized on the first day of our vacation when we're in Florida?" I gulped. We won't be back until Friday." I flipped the phone shut and started kicking sand out in every direction, not caring about who witnessed my infantile fit.

I coached myself. *This will all work out. Everything happens for a reason.* I turned to Lamaze breathing and clenched my toes in and out to the rhythm of the waves to calm down. Rob and I sat next to the pool and watched the kids splash. I sipped a mai tai to chill my nerves, but it didn't help. Apparently, the Universe is a real prankster. Right when I'd given up control and traveled fourteen hundred miles away, my ideal home miraculously appeared. *Am I being punished?*

Clearly, I just didn't trust the Universe or the natural order of events. I'm probably just a recovering control freak, willing to work hard and use blood, sweat, and willpower to get what I want. And although I honestly tried to enjoy my time on the striped, padded blue beach recliner, I never reached a cool state of "Zen." There was no relaxing in the Sunshine State because I had a gnawing desire to get back home.

We flew back Friday morning and the minute we arrived, Beth came knocking. She drove me frantically to a three-story Georgian with two intricately carved Corinthian columns and a cherry red door. I stammered, "This is it! It's my stunning White House across from the lake!" The house sported views of the water from all easterly windows and was located across from a park with rolling hills and a sprawling dog beach. I ran inside. The house had everything I'd requested. The kitchen was cramped and there was only a small side yard, but those features weren't on my original list anyway, so I didn't mind.

In the late afternoon, I drove the family back over to the property's bright crimson doorstep. The children cheered as they ran inside, claiming future bedrooms. I cried out to Beth with elation, "Place a bid immediately for twenty thousand above the asking price!" It was the exact amount for which we'd been approved.

She made a quick phone call to the listing realtor and turned back to face me, stone-cold and white. She choked, "Another family just put a bid on the house and it was accepted."

I died right there inside the elaborate burgundy dining room. This was my palatial mini-mansion! I'd built up my finances and found exactly what I wanted. I threw my head back and moaned, "Put in a backup bid."

Now I really didn't trust the Universe! No, I hated the Universe! Exasperated, I sat on the Georgian steps holding my head in my hands. *All of my time, energy, and persistence had been for nothing.* The other family had a week to schedule an inspection and they could either accept or reject the house of my dreams.

For the following week, I employed every manifestation trick with fervor. Like a stalker, I walked back and forth in front of the elegant house. I stared at the red door and imagined the entertaining parties I'd host inside. I even took my psycho terrier to the dog beach across the street so that the location would feel more real to both of us. But as the days passed, the She-Devil awoke and started writhing inside, hissing words of self-blame. *You're going to stay cramped in that old house forever. This is all your fault. You should have never taken that trip. You didn't deserve it, and look what happened.*

I waited six long days, carrying on with work and family matters, but on the inside, I was awash in agitation. By the evening of the seventh day, it became painfully obvious . . . the phone wasn't going to ring. I dropped my chin in full surrender. I accepted defeat and moved to a place of calm inside my body. *Is this what acceptance feels like?*

Just then, my cell phone buzzed. "Tell me it's mine!" I squealed with delight, not bothering to give Beth a proper salutation.

She heralded, "Congratulations! The other couple removed their offer after the inspection."

This fact probably should have concerned me, but instead I chanted over and over again, "We got the house! It's ours! I can't believe it!"

Then she announced, "There are three other backup offers behind you, so the owners won't take a contingency on your old house."

I chimed with confidence, "That won't be a problem. Our old place is the cheapest real estate in town. I know it will sell quickly."

I sat in the glow of total victory. My American Dream was complete with a stunning home, red convertible, flashy new BCBG suit, and swinging Prada bag. It took over a year, but I had acquired every item on my "I Want" list. And I was starting to understand how the *Creational Code* worked. The Code was simple: all I had to do was focus my mind, articulate a clear and specific request to the Universe, write everything down to seal it, invest my mental and sensory energy toward the topic and apply my best physical effort. And more critically, I detached from the outcome and relaxed. Voila! The object of my desire was delivered. I had become masterful and using the Creational Code to satisfy my materialistic needs.

In massive hurricane-like style, I moved forward and redecorated our new home, painting the front hall in butterscotch hues, adding formal red fleur-de-lis wallpaper throughout and custom colors to each child's room according to his or her specific tastes. In four short weeks, we moved in and I threw an enormous housewarming bash to celebrate our waterside digs. Everything was just right.

I loved my fancy house, and as an extra bonus, I was serendipitously awarded a new marketing project from one of our party guests. I also spent time scouring and painting the old farmhouse, listing it quickly on the market. Life was grand!

≈ 7 ≈

Telepathic Paging

To me, this entrainment phenomenon was an amazingly untapped tool. By now, I was competent at manifesting things, but imagine how powerful I'd become if I became the pony express of psychic paging. Wouldn't it be fun to use mental energy and nonverbal communication to attract other people?

≈

Having accomplished many of my goals, I felt compelled to raise my skills to an even higher level. In Lynne McTaggart's book *The Intention Experiment*, she cites countless scientific experiments illustrating the power of direct mental influence.

In 2005, a group of researchers from Bastyr University and the University of Washington gathered 30 couples with strong emotional and psychological connections and also a great deal of experience in meditation. The pairs were split up and placed in rooms 10 meters away from each other, with an EEG amplifier

wired up to the occipital lobe of the brain . . .
(The study) demonstrated that the brain-wave
response of the sender to the (visual) stimuli is
mirrored in the receiver, and that the stimulus
in the receiver occurs in an identical place in
the brain as that of the sender. The receiver's
brain reacts as though he or she is seeing the
same image at the same time.

—Lynne McTaggart, *The Intention Experiment*

Taggart explains that in many cases, when one person
is sending a direct, focused intention to another person, our
brains become entrained. Our combined thoughts, words,
and intentions travel like waves across a lattice-like web,
touching and connecting to those with whom we've had
contact. This is precisely why, when you simply think about
someone, they typically respond back to you, directly.

To me, this *entrainment* phenomenon was an amazingly untapped tool. By now, I was competent at manifesting things, but imagine how powerful I'd become if I
became the pony express of psychic paging. Wouldn't it
be fun to use mental energy and nonverbal communication to attract other people?

With this notion in mind, I embarked on a new set
of mental experiments. I wanted to deliberately test my
abilities in the area of telepathic messaging to see if I
could get people to respond to their psychic inbox.

I'm a realist, so I know some people are open to the
world of energy. I call these individuals "Energy Receptors." My mother, daughter, and older brother fall into this
category. There are also a group of people who are closed
off from receiving or responding to energetic signals. I call
these folks "Energy Resisters." Individuals in this category

are often psychically shut down. This group includes my father, great-aunt, and several old friends.

Needless to say, I began my experiment with one of the Receptors, my mother. She lives only a few miles away, and typically we'd talk on the phone once a week. I wanted to see if I could get her to call me more often by using thoughts alone, so I took a seat on the porch and quietly paged: *Rita, call me. Rita, call me now.*

By the end of the day, my cell phone rang. "Honey, are you okay?" my mother inquired with concern. This was just too easy. Every time I actively paged, she responded. Mothers and daughters must have an invisible entrainment umbilical cord. The experiment was forcing me to chat with my mom way more than I desired, so I stopped psychically calling her and moved on to a bigger challenge.

Lori and I had been friends for several years. She's a free-flowing woman with a bold will and a successful entrepreneurial contracting business. We were both busy and rarely found time to chat during the day. As part of my grand experiment, I grabbed an old photo of the two of us at a New Year's Eve party, sporting wide-toothed grins. I stared at the picture of her auburn hair and freckled face and sent my friend a mental message. *Lori, call me tomorrow!* The next day I received a text. "Thinking about you, girlfriend. We need to do lunch . . . Lori." I was delighted that she'd received my message and responded so quickly.

For the next month, I expanded my practice and randomly paged different friends and family members. Typically, I'd receive a text message, email, or phone call within a week. My telepathic results had become very consistent, so I decided to increase the difficulty.

I focused on reaching out to an old neighbor whom I'd not seen since we'd moved, months earlier. I thought about her friendly face and two charming young daughters. Mentally, I sent her well wishes and asked her to get in touch with me. Shortly thereafter on my way to the bank, I pulled up to a crosswalk in downtown Winnetka and the woman walked right in front of my car. I hit the horn and waved madly. She approached and I rolled down the window, grinning like the Cheshire Cat. We took a few moments to get reacquainted and secretly, I congratulated myself on yet another successful connection.

The telepathic paging tool also remarkably came in handy when I was cut off from modern telecommunication. On a weekend day, I'd agreed to join two friends for a Meetup group hike at the Waterfall Glen scenic trail in western Illinois, along with eighteen other hikers. Unfortunately, I overslept and ran out of the house an hour late, disheveled, and left my phone on the charger. I sped like an Indy 500 driver down the freeway, but it didn't matter. I arrived at the trailhead an hour late. All the hikers were deep within the woods. Totally disgusted with myself for being tardy and without any communication device, I took a seat on a nearby bench, adjusted my bootlaces, and sighed. I sent a sincere telepathic apology to my friends and asked for their forgiveness.

After a few minutes, I stood up to study the tall, dusty map and prepared myself for a solo journey into the woods. I walked five hundred paces in a westerly direction down a random rocky trail and bumped straight into the arms of my welcoming friends. The other eighteen hikers were four miles into the journey, but by the miracle of synchronicity, my friends had chosen to end their hike early. They cut through the woods on a side path and ran straight into me. The three of us sat munching granola bars, enthusiastically discussing the details of our lives.

~ 8 ~

Old Haunts

*I'm not the kind of person who typically believes in ghosts,
but I walked straight into the middle of the living room to
address the situation directly. I spoke with imposing volume and waved my arms to demonstrate complete authority. "I'm telling you to stop haunting us, walking up stairs,
opening doors, and turning things on and off."*

~

By now, my physical manifestation skills were sharp
and my nonverbal communication prowess was well
established. Unfortunately, our family had a much more
difficult issue to address. After six months, the stucco
farmhouse was still on the market without a single offer.
Even though we'd moved on with our lives, the farmhouse sat empty with a "For Sale" sign tipped toward the
street. The property was spotlessly clean, rooms painted
Navajo white, and the yard pristinely manicured. The
strange part was, other houses in the neighborhood were
selling like hotcakes and ours was the lowest price in
town. After hosting several open houses, Beth informed

me that qualified buyers were running out and never looking back. She simply couldn't understand why.

I began to wonder if something else was wrong with the old place. Nine years earlier, I'd found the house in a local newspaper on sale for $265,000. I'd just finished graduate school and was pregnant for the first time, with Alexandra. So, on a whim, I'd thrown out a super lowball offer and the dwelling was ours, no questions asked. The structure was tiny, but we were delighted to have a place to call home. Strange occurrences, however, started taking place not long after we settled into the Dundee Road homestead.

One day, I asked Rob to take Alexandra out for a walk so I could finish an urgent marketing report. The two of them had been gone for less than fifteen minutes when I heard five loud clomping steps moving slowly down the gray plank basement stairs. I turned around and looked beyond the support beams, to catch a glimpse of who was approaching. I called out, "Rob, is that you?" No answer. I stood up and yelled, "Why are you guys back so soon?" Again, silence. "Is someone in the house?"

I ran to the base of the stairs and looked up, but no one was there. I checked every room in the house before disregarding the incident and quickly forgot that it had ever happened.

Two weeks later, I woke up to the sound of Alexandra crying, in anticipation of her 2:00 a.m. feeding. I entered the nursery with a bottle in hand, closed the door, and picked her up out of the crib with only a dim night-light shining next to me. Just as we sat down together on the rocking chair, the bedroom door burst open and the bright overhead light flipped on. Terrified, I screamed and ran into the hallway, making the poor baby cry. I flew into our bedroom and woke Rob up. He stumbled around the house, checking for intruders. Just like the time before, there was no one else in the house.

The next day, I decided to walk down the street and knock on a few doors to see if I could obtain information regarding the property's history. There, I met a gentleman in his eighties who'd lived on our block since childhood. He told me that ours was the first house to be built in the early 1900s. The front yard had maintained a hitching post and trough with clear, clean water so that weary travelers could tie up their horses and take a rest under the canopy of two large oak trees. At the time, it was owned by the prominent Mr. and Mrs. Clavey, who lived in the house with their children.

Regrettably, in her senior years, Mrs. Clavey had not been well attended and had died of a heart attack in her bedroom. Her body lay stiff for days before anyone reported her missing. The fire department jimmied the lock off the front door to get her body out, and the crowbar cuts were still plainly visible in the wood.

Strange events continued throughout our entire first year at the farmhouse. One evening while the family was seated around the kitchen table eating dinner, the television in the adjoining room turned on by itself. A news program was blaring on the set. I ran over and suspiciously glared at the TV, knowing I'd turned it off before serving the meal. I looked around for the animals to make sure neither the dog nor the cat had accidently stepped on the remote control, but they were nowhere in sight. A few moments later, the kids' electronic toys began speaking out loud unexpectedly. "This is the letter B." "Hi, my name is Elmo." "Q is for *queen*." I scooted over to each toy and cautiously pushed the off button. My body began nervously shuddering. I wondered if an airplane had somehow sent electromagnetic waves into the house, but when I stepped outside to check, the sky was clear.

Although there was no rational explanation for the events that took place inside the Dundee Road homestead, two things were abundantly clear: Our electronics were entertaining themselves, and it was freaking me out.

One day, Alexandra grabbed my arm and pulled me down to her level, whispering fearfully in my ear, "Mommy, make it stop."

I probed, "What? Make what stop?"

She whimpered, "The ghost lady, make her stop." My child's plea motivated me to take matters into my own hands. I'm not the kind of person who typically believes in ghosts, but I walked straight into the middle of the living room to address the situation directly. I spoke with imposing volume and waved my arms to demonstrate complete authority. "I'm telling you to stop haunting us, walking up stairs, opening doors, and turning things on and off. It's scaring my family. Thank you!" I walked out of the room and wiggled my shoulders to release the tension. Strangely, my request paid off. The noises stopped in the house for almost three years as we added a new member to our family, Emma.

When Alexandra was a five-year-old fantasy-loving girl and Emma still a toddler, we scheduled an outing to the Bristol Renaissance Faire in Wisconsin. We loaded into the car, dressed in proper attire from the 1700s, with regal purple velvet gowns, capes, and crowns. Even Rob wore an outfit fit for a king. We took off, singing *Barney* songs and traveling north for an hour-long journey.

Somewhere over the Wisconsin border, I felt chills rushing down my back. Intuitively, I knew something was seriously wrong. I turned and looked at Rob in horror, squeaking, "Stop the car! We need to go back home!" He grimaced and pulled over onto the dusty shoulder. I continued, "It probably sounds crazy, but I just received a mental message that our house is burning down." Rob and the kids stared at me, dumbfounded. But this warning was just too strong to ignore.

Rob swung the car around and we drove all the way back home in complete silence. We walked inside the kitchen and beheld a shocking sight: A cookbook had fallen onto the toaster-oven switch. The small appliance had been running on high for over an hour and the wooden window frame below was charred and burning. I'm not sure how or why I'd received such a strong intuitive notification, but if we'd spent the entire day in Wisconsin, the house would have surely caught fire.

Somehow, I wondered if Mrs. Clavey, the potential ghost inside our house, had tried to communicate with me. In gratitude, I thanked the Universe for keeping us safe. And oddly, the strange sounds and electronic noises started up again in the house and continued until the day we moved.

After we were settled in our new home in Winnetka, the farmhouse morphed into a dark dwelling with cold gusts of air moving through its empty, sterile rooms. A force within the house felt hostile and I was concerned that prospective buyers could feel the heavy, toxic energy. I wondered if Mrs. Clavey felt abandoned and didn't want to embrace a new family inside "her" four walls.

In frustration, I picked up the phone and called an old friend, Nancy. She had battled a similar unfriendly entity years earlier. She listened to my story intently and shared, "If you really want to sell the house, you need to get in touch with the ghost directly and show her to the nearest hospital. That way, she can go to the place where beings enter and exit the world."

I whined, "I just want to sell the house before it financially ruins us. I don't want to have a séance." Nancy snorted at my ignorance and continued to deliver full, detailed instructions.

As my friend had directed, I drove to our empty farmhouse and sat down on the bare living-room floor, uneasily wringing my hands in preparation for human-to-ghost communication. The wood creaked underneath me as I started my speech. "I'm truly sorry, but we'll probably need to sell this land to a developer. If we do that, the house will be torn down." I felt a squeeze of anger across my neck and a pinch in my shoulder. I pointed in a southerly direction. "You can go to the hospital and find a new body or pass over to the other side. The choice is yours, but if there's something I can do to help, let me know."

Suddenly, a clear message dropped into my mind: *Take me to the hospital.*

I clenched my jaw. *Oh God. I think she wants a ride!* Although it seemed totally insane, I paused and carefully considered my options: drive back and forth to the hospital tonight or get stuck with this old property forever. Fortunately, I'd scheduled a babysitter, so I was free for a strange road trip.

I went back to our home in Winnetka and pensively grilled some cheese sandwiches for the kids' dinner. I also took this opportunity to unenthusiastically tell Rob about my evening plans. "I know it sounds nuts, but tonight I have to drive from our old house to the hospital because that's the only way I can get rid of the potential ghost.

But you can't laugh or make fun of this little expedition. It's very serious!"

He burst out chortling, "Are you kidding me?" I gave him a daunting stare and he reluctantly agreed to be my chauffeur. He said, "I'll drive the car, just in case you've completely lost your mind."

We showed up at the vacant house around 9:00 p.m. and walked into the kitchen for a final visit. I loudly announced, "It's time to go. We're driving to the place where all my children were born." I felt a surge of heaviness as I climbed into the backseat of the car. I sat down and closed my eyes. In my mind's eye I saw vivid black-and-white movie-like scenes of two young boys dressed in tan knickers and leather suspenders. I saw dirt roads, farms, horses, and a few frame houses near the train station. I shuddered.

When we arrived at the hospital, a guard met us at the front door, authoritatively announcing, "I'm sorry, visiting hours are over. You'll need to come back tomorrow."

Rob and I turned around and slowly walked outside, taking a seat on the cold stone bench in front of the medical institution. I closed my eyes tightly and sent the ghost encouraging thoughts, pointing my index finger toward the maternity ward. The hairs stood straight up on my outstretched arm. Rob announced in an eerie tone, "She's gone now."

I popped my eyes open and inquired, "How do you know?" He gestured toward the large double glass sliding doors twenty feet away. "The hospital doors opened and closed all by themselves and no one was there." As you might have guessed, we sold the old house two days later. This is a true story.

9

Bridging the Power

*In my spare time, I developed a training program to help
people manifest their true desires. Now, I just needed to
find a willing lab partner, someone who was open and
receptive to a powerful new way of thinking. It was 2003
and several years before* The Secret *popularized the
concept of "manifesting," so finding a New Age student
wasn't particularly easy.*

~

A fter selling the old house, everything moved forward with a pleasant hum. I was living the life most
people only dreamed of, the one you see in the movies
before all the drama hits. I had a house on Mansion Row,
three flourishing kids, a fit figure, and a sassy convertible.
With so many marketing contracts, the flow of cash made
me feel positively euphoric.

I was able to hire a nanny four days per week to take
care of the children and I felt fully supported for the first
time, ever. Dominica was a sturdy, bossy, capable Eastern
European woman who spoke broken English and quickly

became my perfect wife. I rented a small office nearby and came home every evening to a clean, bubbling household and a fragrant home-cooked Polish dinner.

Busy, but not overwhelmed, I decided to impulsively fulfill yet another childhood fantasy. I purchased Rose, a lively four-year-old dark bay Thoroughbred mare with a clean white blaze straight down the center of her nose. I'd ridden horses since childhood and figured that regularly exercising a twelve-hundred-pound animal would help me keep the weight off.

Having found such personal satisfaction through manifesting, I also had a burning desire to share my abilities with others. In my spare time, I developed a training program to help people manifest their true desires. Now, I just needed to find a willing lab partner, someone who was open and receptive to a powerful new way of thinking. It was 2003, years before *The Secret* popularized New Age concepts, so finding a student wasn't particularly easy.

I needed to find someone objective, a person who really wanted to learn life-altering skills. Therefore, I turned my attention to my client base. During long marketing meetings, I searched for key opportunities to shift business conversations into something more personal. Coffee breaks seemed like the perfect times to ask more meaningful questions: "What do you do for fun?" "What are your favorite activities?" "What kinds of things do you love to participate in?"

I discovered that my business associates were more than willing to fervently share such information. They sat up tall and leaned forward with a bright light shining from their eyes. It was like asking a child what they wanted from Santa. Everyone answered enthusiastically, expressing their long-repressed dreams: "I would love to be a yoga teacher." "I'm in the middle of writing a mystery novel." "I've always wanted to open an organic gardening business."

I heard joyful stories about singing in a madrigal choir, coaching little league baseball, and playing the bass guitar. Sadly, I also heard about the disappointment and regrets that accompanied neglecting these soul-driven interests.

One day after a long branding session, Randy, a health-care marketer, stopped me in the hallway. He'd overheard a conversation I'd had with another co-worker regarding the topic of true purpose. He spoke in a hushed voice. "Dianne, I'm ready to make changes. I want to achieve my genuine goals and fix my life."

I took this to be a Brass Ring Moment and I immediately shot back, "I can help you. I'm working on developing services to assist people in changing their lives. Do you want free manifestation consulting?"

For a second, Randy squinted at me as if I were an alien. Then he gushed, "Yes, absolutely. I'm your man."

I was thrilled: I'd found my guinea pig! We shook hands and met the following week at the Half Moon Diner for an early-morning breakfast. The restaurant was conveniently located on the south side of a busy divided highway and looked more like a truck stop than a fine-dining establishment. I'd known Randy in a professional capacity for two years, but really, I knew very little about him. I began our first meeting by laying out "The Shortcuts for Living Well" and imparting specific techniques for effective manifestation. I also highlighted my personal success stories and failures. Randy listened intently, scribbling down notes between bites of dry, overly toasted bagel.

It was time to turn the tables, so I invited Randy to share with me details of his life's journey. He didn't waste any time. "For the past ten years, I thought I had the perfect existence. As you know, I've been a regional sales manager, and although my job has required regular travel, I was happily married to my soul mate, Marie. Together, we had been raising two wonderful daughters."

Randy told me he wholeheartedly believed that his wife had cherished her role as a stay-at-home mom. This unfortunately, was far from the truth. Marie felt trapped, stagnant, and alone. She longed to find romance and excitement and ventured out into the arms of another man, a longtime family friend. She carried on an intense affair for several months until she could no longer bear the deception.

One day, after Randy returned from a weeklong sales conference, Marie came clean. "I'm in love with someone else. I want a divorce and need to take some time to find myself. And, I don't want to be the main caregiver anymore for our kids." Suddenly and without warning, he was a single parent.

Randy sat across from me, his brows tightly knit, tensely rubbing his fingers along a stained coffee mug. This staggering event had happened six months earlier, and he assured me the initial shock was over. He'd taken steps to regain control of his rocky life: filed for divorce, found a nanny to take care of the children, and Marie had moved in with her lover. With these intense family changes, however, Randy could no longer travel, and as a result, his job was in jeopardy. Plus, his body was racked with pain from the daunting stress.

The man held his voice steady as he beseeched, "Dianne, I need to start over. I'm ready to move on and create a better life." I heard his rational words but saw something else. Across from me was a man overwhelmed by desertion and betrayal. A dump truck had pulled up and poured his life into a cone of dirt right on top of his head. This was complete upheaval. I assured Randy that although transformation was often not enjoyable, it was usually a critical part of personal growth. I gave him a few manifestation exercises and we agreed to meet again at the Half Moon the following week.

Randy was a committed and diligent student. I provided the rules, framework, and tools, and he devoted the time and energy to the work. We met frequently over the next few months and he made astounding progress, interviewing for several non-travel positions and landing the ideal lateral management job with regular business hours.

This man also found a new base of personal power. He attended physical therapy sessions to soothe his aching back, lightened up his outlook, and ventured out on evenings off to enjoy being a single man. He started going out on dates and within a few months met a delightful woman at a mixer. She was also divorced, had two children, and was ready to start her life anew. The couple quickly fell in love and shortly thereafter began making plans to integrate their mini Brady Bunch–like family.

I beamed with joy. Randy's enormous courage was an inspiration to me and I couldn't believe how rapidly his transformation took place. Plus, I was tickled to see my process at work.

~

SECTION IV

Modern Family, Secret Separation

~

10

Chasm of the Heart

Everyone knew therapy wasn't going to solve our marital problem. We didn't have that kind of money and Rob and I didn't have what it took for a husband-and-wife relationship, period, end of story. We left knowing change was imminent.

∽

In the months to come, I'd often think about Randy and the manner in which his life imploded. Yet, what I didn't know at the time was that my life was also on a harrowing crash course.

When Rob and I first had bought the starter-mansion, my business was strong and my lifestyle rich. I was Wonder Woman, raising gold cuffs, soaring though the air with the aid of a dainty blue cape. Unfortunately, I missed the memo stating, "Big houses equal big expenses." It might sound Pollyanna-ish, even dumb, but I was surprised when the guts of the Georgian began breaking down at a rapid pace. The gas stove leaked toxic fumes, the water heater spit out lukewarm streams, the garage roof seeped precipitation down the walls, and three inches of mucky silt poured into the laundry room after every rain. Is this what they call a "money pit"?

I walked uneasily around our breathtakingly appointed domicile, concerned about my materialist choices. I began to fear for our financial future. By mid-2004 the economy had still not recovered from the shock of 9/11 and business professionals were continuing to get laid off, many of whom were my clients. Also, since we'd carried double mortgages for so long, our savings account was nearly dried up. As a quick maneuver for emergency cash, Rob and I ran to the bank and were approved for a second mortgage, just in case we needed it. Reluctantly and with massive consternation, I also let Dominica go.

The stress of tightening our belts and losing the nanny triggered an avalanche of marital issues. For the past twelve years, Rob and I had perfected the art of duty-driven cohabitant living. He was the part-time butler and I was the full-time Molly McMaid.

While hunting for business deals, I simultaneously managed the agenda of every person and animal in our clan, including play dates, sporting events, doctor visits, field trips, lunch duty, shopping, house repairs, cleaning, laundry, dog walking, horse shoeing, and all social functions. This laborious "task overwhelm" triggered one of my most prevalent behavioral patterns: the Queen of Burden. I was the good cop and the bad cop, the fun-loving mom and the chore master, the playmate and the disciplinarian. I organized everything and told everyone else what to do. And, when Rob came home from his graphic design job, he took out the trash and planted the flowers. Herein lay the problem.

According to another one of Sonia's recommended books, *Intimate Communion*, Rob and I suffered from backward male/female polarity.

> After asking hundreds of educated and successful women and men to make these lists at workshops across the United States, I have found that the results are amazingly consistent from city to city. What emerges are lists of qualities that describe the ideal man or woman, the intimate partner of our fantasies.
>
> These lists of qualities have very little overlap. Women and men want distinctly different qualities in their intimate partners. This is to be expected. After all, most (but not all) of us have a preference: we want to be sexually intimate with a person who is more Masculine or Feminine.
>
> —David Deida, *Intimate Communion*

I was the driver of our lives and Rob tended to the plants. I openly blame this on the women's lib generation. When I was a child, our society was grooming strong, independent businesswomen. Girls were taught to leave the kitchen behind and evolve into ball-busting corporate executives who break glass ceilings.

I'll always remember Charles of the Ritz's popular 1980 Enjoli advertising campaign targeted toward young impressionable females like me, which poetically declared that women could bring home the bacon, fry it up, and never let their men forget they were men!

If I'm not mistaken, this means women take responsibility for everything from making tons of money during the day to ensuring that their menfolk are "pleased" at night. Oh, and by the way, while wives are multitasking, who's watching the children? I guess they get outsourced.

According to *Intimate Communion*, most women subconsciously want their men to be leaders, solid decision-makers, and drivers in the partnership.

> Virtually every woman agreed that foremost among all the qualities they wanted in their man were: 1. Presence 2. Intelligence 3. Strength 4. Passion 5. Direction 6. Humor.
>
> —David Deida, *Intimate Communion*

I would happen to agree with this list. And men want their women to be open, loving, and exquisitely receptive in the glow of the relationship. I am not a man, but I can only assume that this too is true.

> The qualities that men across the country wanted most in their women were: 1. Beauty 2. Sexual openness 3. Trust of their (man's) direction 4. Support for their (man's) vision 5. Healthy radiance.
>
> —David Deida, *Intimate Communion*

At the Hoffman Institute, I worked hard to reconnect to my essence. I fixed the gaping hole in my self-esteem and found an enormous capacity for self-love. Rob also attended Hoffman shortly after Adam was born and he too experienced personal growth. Disappointingly, even Hoffman couldn't address our core issue, an enormous lack of impassioned union.

I vividly recall my wedding day, standing in the vestibule of the church. Most women are ecstatic and thrilled to become someone's wife, thinking about the magical ceremony, the kiss, and the cake. I wasn't thinking about any of that. I remember nervously fidgeting with the satin flowers on my long ivory gown, scanning my brain for ways to cancel the wedding without having my German-bred father kill me. I didn't want to get married, but I knew I couldn't pay him back the twenty thousand dollars he'd just invested in my "glorious" event.

I felt trapped, as if I were being forced to follow an unspoken social edict to wed. Right before I took my dad's arm and began the formal stroll down the aisle, I whispered with a timbre of dread, "Can I go home now?" He brusquely barked, "As soon as the ceremony is over!" So that was it. I walked straight down the aisle at twenty-eight, but my heart was nowhere to be found.

Sonia had given me the specific task of finding my heart, but I never had gooey feelings for my husband and I couldn't fabricate them. *What's wrong with me? Perhaps love doesn't exist. Maybe this lifetime I'll be reduced to wearing a chore-driven yoke.*

The She-Devil woke up and professed doom from the crypt, coating my mind with abysmal notions: *Love is a pipe dream. Passion doesn't exist. It's all hogwash. Your heart will never feel warm because love isn't real anyway.* Wait a minute! These words were dimly familiar. I'd heard them before, but from where? Nonetheless, I knew they were untrue. When I was seventeen I'd found "Summer Lovin'," just like in the movie *Grease*, so I figured love had to be real.

At the end of my junior year in high school, I'd settled into Chicago and searched for a summer job to avoid sitting all day in a boring house. With very few demonstrable skills, I applied to the only "Help Wanted" sign in town, a Woolworth five-and-dime. I was gainfully employed as a waitress and grill cook. Yes, I flipped burgers at a vinyl-covered dining counter located inside a small retail store.

I wore a starched pink polyester dress with white lace fringe and a hairnet. I found an old name badge in a drawer that said MADGE and pinned it to my outfit. My boss went along with the joke. I really hated cooking, but figured flipping flapjacks on the griddle was better than sitting at home, so I mastered the art of grilling, deep-fat frying, and blending.

Much to my surprise, the job came with a huge benefit. One day, the gods took pity on me and sent a stunning vision of loveliness to my dining counter. With celestial music playing above and rays of sunshine bursting from his shiny auburn hair, Jim sat down on the small stool and threw me a sparkling smile. I just stood there, rock-still.

Right in front of me sat a handsome, chiseled young man with piercing cobalt blue eyes. The Universe had made my day! Jim was a college student working in Chicago for the summer. He wore dusty work boots and held a construction sign, the kind that said STOP on one side and SLOW on the other. It wasn't an impressive job, but after all, I was playing the role of "Madge," the short-order chef, so I was in no position to judge.

Jim asked me what was tasty on the menu and then proceeded to eat every bite of my freshly fried burger. He must have enjoyed the fattening cuisine because he came to my counter for lunch every day that week.

By Friday, as I was in the middle of draining Tater Tots, Jim shot out the blessed question. "Can I take you to dinner sometime, Madge?"

I whisked off my hairnet, wiped the grease off of my hands, and tried to act cool. "Yeah, sure, that would be nice. My name is Dianne." He looked up at me and tipped his head like a confused puppy.

Underneath the utility vest, he behaved like a brilliant young university professor, debating heavy philosophical issues and speaking in four-syllable words. He became my Harlequin romance, weaving eloquent *amour* sonnets as we strolled around the neighborhood after work holding hands, looking intently into each other's gaze. It was "first love" for both of us, innocent and sublime. Our relationship grew and blossomed over the balmy summer months and my heart literally broke into a million pieces the day Jim returned to Florida State University. A part of me died that day; sadly, we were just too young to start a life together.

I sat in my room bawling for weeks, unable to function without the boy who made me feel whole and complete. After too many "annoying tears," my father stormed in and bellowed the following words to make me shut up: "You think you loved him, except that was puppy love. You don't know what love is. Real love is about work. Nothing else exists." These words etched their way into my subconscious as my father marched out and Jim's tearstained letters ceased. In my adult life and especially in marriage, I'd never again felt the magnitude of such impassioned closeness.

As a woman determined to reignite her quintessence, marriage had become a weighty cloud, a gnashing, gnawing monster. Instead of sharing laughter and affection, Rob and I focused on the resentment of the grind. I snapped drill-sergeant orders to make him contribute at a higher level. "Watch the kids while I work on a proposal."

"Grab the dirty clothes from the bathroom." "Don't be late when you pick the girls up from piano lessons." "Change Adam's dirty training pants and, for God's sake, take down the darn Christmas lights. It's March!" As my autocratic behavior escalated, so did Rob's resistance to household assistance.

According to marital relationship experts, couples fight most frequently over the following topics: money, work, kids, housework, and sex. Rob and I covered the gamut. We argued about the mortgage, our reduced income, paying the bills, child-care responsibilities, endless tasks, and lack of intimacy. One day after an enormous financial spat, I quipped, "There are plenty of bedrooms in this house. Why don't you just move your stuff upstairs into the guest room so you don't keep waking me up with your infernal snoring?"

He apathetically retorted, "Fine, whatever." And that was it. Rob moved his belongings into the third floor.

Despite our crumbling relationship, the kids were blissfully unaware of our marital trouble. Best of all, I had a serene space to myself. I knew it was a bad omen, but after Rob moved out of the bedroom, I felt giddy. I looked around at my meticulously appointed private master suite, Jacuzzi, walk-in closet, and dainty sitting parlor. I was thrilled with the blessed sanctuary in what I now affectionately called my "apartment."

As the months passed, my relationship with Rob continued to dissolve. We scooted sideways past each other in the hall, avoiding contact. Everything about him annoyed me, everything he did, and especially everything he didn't do. Eventually, I just perceived him as a lazy, good-for-nothing bum. Instead of expressing our overwhelming feelings of dejection for a marriage that was spiraling out of control, we moved toward disdain, hurl-ing negative verbal fireballs of frustration and then run-ning away to the protection of our private rooms.

I took meditative walks along the beach, searching for enlightenment or a bit of direction from above. I pon-dered the concept of divorce, but a quilt of shame over-whelmed me. *Loving mothers and fathers don't hurt their kids; my job is to be a guardian for these three gorgeous children. Perhaps when Adam is out of high school, I can take a bold step and move out on my own. But by then, I'll be over sixty.*

While preparing to skip a perfectly flat stone, I stopped dead in my tracks. An image from childhood popped into mind. I saw a picture of my mother and father living in different parts of the house. They too had the ultimate utilitarian relationship and commu-nicated through loud, angry bursts. This was my worst nightmare! What had I done? Was I subconsciously play-ing out scenes from my past?

I was terrified to be a single mom, living alone, work-ing all the time, unable to pay the bills, with only a cat to heat up my bed. Hold on a minute! Wasn't that what I'd already created? I was forty-two with three small chil-dren, living in a private bedroom with Simon, a hairy dreamsicle-colored feline at my feet. Our entire house-hold was tightly bound together with duty as our glue.

After tiptoeing around the house for what seemed like an eternity, I couldn't stuff the unhappiness any lon-ger. I finally found the courage to articulate what neither of us could bear to divulge after twelve years together. I cornered Rob in the hallway and calmly announced, "I can't do this anymore. This isn't a marriage and I want out of whatever 'this' is." He just stood there, looking at his shoes, nodding. For the first time in half a year, we agreed on something: Cohabitation wasn't working. And we agreed upon one more thing: last-ditch marriage counseling.

I called Sonia's office and received the name of Leslie, an experienced couple's counselor. Rob and I arrived at her office in separate cars. The therapist was an attractive bohemian-style woman with long flowing hair, a purple flowery skirt, and boots. We settled quietly into her plush mauve armchairs and shared with her an overview of our relationship. Leslie bent forward, eagerly anticipating our tale, searching for the root of the problem. Much to her surprise, we didn't have a chest of covert deeds or lies; there was no drug abuse, drinking problems, gambling, swinging, or prostitutes. We had nothing to confess except a huge chasm of the heart, one the size of the Grand Canyon.

After hearing our story the therapist asked us to participate in several exercises to reveal our innermost feelings. I called the first exercise the "I Hate It When Game." Each individual is allowed to state everything they hate about their current living situation including job, personal relationships, annoying habits, partner's idiosyncrasies, and even the weather. The other person has to sit attentively and listen until the first party is fully expressed.

Rob went first. It took him only a second to start hurling an intricate list of "hates" into the tiny office and of course it was all about me. He hated my endless drive, nagging, temper, dictatorial mannerisms, chores, lack of appreciation, biting words, insomnia, the way I squeezed the toothpaste, the streaks of mascara down my face in the morning, and my incompetence at loading the dishwasher. In a nutshell, he hated most of the qualities that comprised my personality.

I absorbed his words. Somehow the exercise seemed clarifying and informative rather than hurtful. I found it enlightening to hear Rob express his intense aggravation, even if I was the subject. When he finished venting, it was my job to succinctly repeat his list of complaints to make sure I'd grasped every utterance. I did exactly that.

Then it was my turn. I sat for a moment, afraid to unleash my hideous truth. This was something I'd brilliantly hidden for over a decade. I really didn't want to dump a pile of steamy dog poop on the shag carpet below me. I warned Leslie, "I don't think I should do this." But the therapist firmly insisted, so I lifted the guard gate off my tongue.

"I hate Rob's inactivity around the house, personal limits, immature nature, babyish reactions, childishness, road rage, lack of initiative, and the way he loudly slurps every sip of coffee. The real problem is, he's the indolent household teenager and I'm his obnoxious, nagging mother. I hate his passive personality and I haven't been attracted to him in years. We are like two polar magnets flipping in endless circles; the North and South Pole will never get together."

Wow, it felt amazing to get to the bottom of "My Hate" pool. Nevertheless, when I stopped tossing out words, I saw Rob huddled in the over-stuffed therapy chair, shoulders sunken. He was crushed.

The therapist quickly presented us with a second exercise. I called this one the "Verbal Ink Blot." She instructed, "Close your eyes and make your mind blank. When I ask you a question, simply throw out the first response that bubbles up from the gut. Don't censor or filter anything, just blurt."

Leslie calmly probed, "In your perfect world, Rob, how would this relationship with Dianne work?" With eyes tightly shut, Rob described a scene from a Gene Kelly musical with the two of us tap dancing up the staircase of life and swaying in eternal joy.

Then, it was my turn. The image that gelled in my mind wasn't as pretty. I popped both eyes open, giving the therapist a "you don't want to hear this" kind of look. She beat me down with an intense pressure-filled stare and I caved. "Rob would live next door and the kids move back and forth between our homes." I heard a small gasp from the other side of the room, but my long-repressed veracious flow continued, "I haven't felt love inside me for years. I don't want to be married."

As our session came to a close, the therapist recommended weekly counseling sessions at two hundred dollars per hour. All three of us stood there in her doorway, shaking hands, expressionless. Everyone knew therapy wasn't going to solve our marital problem. We didn't have that kind of money and Rob and I didn't have what it took for a husband-and-wife relationship, period, end of story. We left knowing change was imminent.

With such clarity, you'd think I'd move quickly toward a divorce. Wrong, I did not. Although I'd expressed my desire for freedom, I came up with a million reasons to drag my feet: I had nothing figured out. Money was tight. I was scared to be out on my own and definitely didn't want to hurt the kids. Quite selfishly, I also didn't want to leave my comfy residential masterpiece.

There are very few social models for handling marital separation creatively. So, the day after our therapy session, I retreated to my "apartment" to figure out what to do next. I started by asking myself a few coaching questions. *If you were not afraid of anything, what would the next phase of this family-life look like? What would give you a sense of peacefulness and calm?*

My mind's eye envisioned a "family house" in which Rob and I continued to share the property, raise the children, and pay the bills together, but nothing else. Both parties could move on, but no one would move out. It was an ideal modern scenario for postponing the ugliness of divorce, school-hallway whispers, financial ruin, and of even greater consequence, the children's grief. Come to think of it, we'd been living a similar model for the past six months, so we were already ahead of the game.

I ran off to locate Rob. He was alone in the kitchen, having poured a fresh glass of milk and looking forlorn. Sheepishly I approached, "What do you think of this idea . . . we'll separate, but continue to live here together, just like we do now. We'll split the bills and the time required to care for the kids. That way, we don't have to rush and put the house up for sale. We can figure out how we both want to move forward."

I shrank back and waited for a response. Rob's shoulders sagged as he lowered his glass to the counter. I could tell he was relieved when he dropped his head into his hands and vigorously shook it up and down. We also agreed on another critical point, not to tell the children about our separation until we had a concrete plan for the future.

I scurried out of the kitchen to type up a facsimile parenting agreement, outlining a child-care schedule. Rob took off in the other direction to prepare a do-it-yourself separation agreement. I'm not sure exactly how it happened, but I'd managed to get separated with a minimal amount of distress or embarrassment.

≈ 11 ≈

Cougar Living

*Over the next few months, I established a rare and fasci-
nating double life. By day, I was a focused, hardworking
suburban mother of three. By night, I was a single woman
experiencing the pulse of one of the world's liveliest cities.*

≈

In the weeks that followed, I joyfully swooned, knowing I was no longer a suburban-housewife prisoner. I
felt different, lighter. Nothing had changed, and yet
everything had changed. I stepped forth from my former
marital cage and approached the world with the curiosity of a child. I also found something I'd been missing for
decades, the most precious of all commodities: time. Rob
and I had been taking turns watching the kids, so I threw
myself back into auditioning with gusto.

Two years of acting classes and private vocal training
finally paid off. I joyfully landed the lead role of Sister in
the production of *Damn Yankees!* That was it! I'd made it
to the top of the community theater heap. I felt as if I'd
been nominated for an Academy Award. Weeks flew by
as I rehearsed—acting, singing, and dancing my feet off.

Night after night, a perfectionist director worked us hard, running rehearsals late. To let off some steam, the cast gathered afterward for snacks and kibitzing. One evening, I caught myself staring a little too long at a young cast mate who was single. I felt a pang of attraction. *That guy is really cute!* I chuckled at my own silliness. *I have three kids living in a secretly separated household.* I corralled the forbidden cognition. *After all, he's much younger than me.* I turned my attention back to the group gossip about our seemingly bipolar director.

The curtain dropped on closing night and I took a final bow after a successful run, sniveling like a teenager at graduation. I cherished my experiences with a leading role and knew I'd miss my newfound thespian friends. I packed up my makeup bag, hung up my costume, and went to sit alone in my office because it was Rob's night to watch the kids.

I had nothing to do and a giant gaping hole in my schedule. I was friendless in one of the most boring places on earth: the suburbs. We lived in Winnetka, Illinois, where restaurateurs sweep their chairs upside down and start mopping at 9:00 p.m., and the only evening entertainment is a shopping-mall movie theater. I was surrounded by Escalade-driving Barbies with bubble-gum-colored lip gloss, permanently bleached teeth, designer sunglasses, highlighted ponytails neatly tucked through baseball caps, diamond studs, and gluteus-hugging black yoga pants. You've seen women like these on sitcoms. I didn't fit into this married, paddle-tennis-playing scene.

I faced reality. On one hand, I was a covertly separated middle-aged woman with three kids living in a mini-mansion with her soon-to-be ex-husband. On the other hand, I had a huge shiny spark for life. In my neighborhood, single women with "family houses" didn't exist.

After college, I'd moved straight to Phoenix, Arizona, to spend time working in commercial real estate. I hung out with girlfriends in two-stepping bars and met young men in church groups. There weren't any church groups for me now.

One evening while sitting in my coffin-quiet office, I surfed the web and clicked on a link that read "Chicago single women in their 40s." I found a host of matchmaking services, networking groups, and the infamous dating machine: Match.com. I couldn't control myself. I entered the site like a driver rubbernecking at a car crash. I felt like a voyeur poking through the bushes at night, peering dangerously into a stranger's window. I scoured the gallery of available men including height, build, habits, interests, and health history. It turned me on and scared me at the same time. I stopped with a jolt. I'd been married for twelve years and I didn't want to start a relationship with a stranger from a website. I slammed my computer shut.

There had to be some way to enjoy my freedom. I turned my thoughts back to the manifestation process. I articulated a new goal. "I want to meet a girlfriend, a guide, someone who is intelligent, reliable, and pleasant with similar creative interests who enjoys having fun. Basically, I need a BFF. Thank you."

In a matter of weeks, three mint-green pineapples landed in the windows of the slot machine; the Universe gave me a gift. At a local Hoffman-sponsored event, I casually announced that I was single and looking forward to meeting new people. A woman stood up, walked straight over to me. Carrie was a medical sales representative, conservative, intelligent, fit, well-dressed, and lived downtown. Best of all, she was the living, breathing guide to Chicago's single life.

Carrie knew everything about where to go and what to do: the picnics for noshing, balls for mingling, music festivals for dancing, street fairs for volunteering, and clubs for socializing. She answered my questions and promptly booked out my calendar. This was the Brass Ring Moment in which I became Carrie's willing, doe-eyed wing-girl. She was the answer to my prayer and I was beyond ecstatic!

Over the next few months, I established a rare and fascinating double life. By day, I was a focused, hardworking suburban mother of three. By night, I was a single woman, experiencing the pulse of one of the world's liveliest cities. On my evenings off, I slid into a fitted outfit, sassy shoes, and cruised down Lake Shore Drive with the wind blowing in my freshly styled hair. Together, Carrie and I spent countless evenings dining, dancing, and having a fantastic time. We ate brats at German Fest, saw movies in the park, played volleyball at the beach, and watched the Cubs lose multiple games in a row, as expected.

Through her, I also met a vivacious group of single friends including Dante, Chicago's unofficial social director. Dante was an attractive half-Filipino/half-Irish man and a talented networker who brought single, forty-something adults together for monthly events. Dante and I also shared a love for the written word. We forged a long-term friendship and met weekly as "writing buddies" to crank the keys on stories that had been gathering dust in our heads. He worked on his screenplay while I began chronicling the tales of my midlife transformation.

And, the best part about my singlehood was that I discovered something new: the real me. I was naturally exuberant and lighthearted. I couldn't stop laughing, anticipating each downtown adventure with glee. I woke up every day feeling energized with the flush of well-being. There it was, exactly what Esther Hicks had been describing.

As I continued to venture out, something strange happened. Single men were passing up single beauties to ask me out on dates. Even though I was older and had a strange living arrangement, my stats didn't seem to matter because I was bubbly and had no pressing biological clock. It just goes to prove that attitude really is everything. Regardless, I politely passed up countless dinner engagements because I was having way too much fun gallivanting around. I didn't want to be tied down.

One evening, my brother passed along two tickets to *The Cherry Orchard*, Chekhov's classic at the Steppenwolf Theatre. Carrie wasn't available, so I picked up the phone and called Tom, an old theater friend. He was an in-your-face, brutally honest, stocky Irishman with speckled green eyes and dancing feet. He personified strength and virility with a salesman-like confidence and was also the same man I'd had a crush on during the play.

I could tell he was thrilled to hear from me because Tom jumped on my ticket offer before I even mentioned the name of the show. We met at a convenient location, I hopped in his car, and we maintained a lively conversation during the long rush-hour drive downtown.

As the lights dimmed on the Steppenwolf stage, I accidently put my arm on the rest next to Tom's muscular forearm. I felt a jolt, a spike of electricity jumping from his limb to mine. I jerked away as if I'd been shot by an electrode. *What was that?* I rubbed my skin. My pulse was racing. I put my elbow back on the armrest and focused on the dramatic *The Cherry Orchard* scene in front of me.

Moments later, I accidentally brushed Tom's arm again and a shock wave of hot sparks slipped down my fingers. I felt a flutter in my chest. What was this mystery tingle? Why am I having unfamiliar palpitations? My brain warned, *Run away. Danger! Forbidden! This tingling is wrong.*

Tom must have also experienced the electrons flying because his shoulders tensed and he smirked with the edges of his mouth. We didn't speak a word during the play, but my physical body was abuzz. I don't remember anything about the production of Chekhov's classic, but I'll never forget my raging pulse and the ache in my base chakra.

When the play ended, Tom and I bantered about our next destination. He was one of seven Irish children and had a natural command of life. He led me to a little disco on Rush Street, tenderly kissed my hand, dragging me onto the dance floor and pulling me close. With the prowess of Fred Astaire, he began spinning and twirling me gracefully as we moved together to the thundering beat of "I Will Survive."

For those magical minutes, I was Cinderella in the arms of a young prince; our gazes locked as we traveled across the tile. Other dancers spontaneously moved back, creating an impromptu dance circle. For his final move, Tom completed a series of fast turns and dipped me slowly to the ground. We continued to hug while moving in a theatrical circle. The crowd clapped wildly. He took my breath away.

In that moment, I begged the Universe to give me the chance to explore these hot, popping feelings inside. My heart was not dead, because I could feel it beating, booming, real and unmistakable.

That evening, Tom and I drove home awkwardly, listening to the radio to avoid direct conversation. He pulled up next to my vehicle and tapped his fingers on the steering wheel. I too hesitated, not wanting this magical night to end. Then he did the unthinkable. He turned toward me and whispered with eternal boldness, "I see the little girl in you. You are a sixteen-year-old, wanting and needing desperately to be held." I gasped.

This man saw right through me! He spoke with unabashed honesty and no fear; he didn't have a filter. Tom got out of the car, walked to the other side, and opened my door. I stood up, my nerves quivering as he cooed, "You're beautiful." He then gave me a long, tight hug. My caged heart was set free. I felt the flame of true love again for the first time since I was a teen.

For the next few weeks, Tom and I spoke regularly on the phone, and in a matter of weeks we were dating. Through him, I experienced an amorous and intimate union. I walked in the clouds and floated throughout the day, enraptured. This relationship showed me everything I'd been missing: romantic chemistry, commitment, strength, virility, and creativity.

Journal Entry

Last night something magical happened. Tom reached for me and gave me the longest, most powerful embrace. He put his hand on the back of my neck and I began to shake lightly. I moved around within his arms from pose to pose, each one feeling warmer than the embrace before. He chuckled and lifted me off the ground, swinging us in a circle. He is so young, playful, and safe. He made me feel twenty pounds lighter and twenty years younger.

Tom backed up slowly and sat down on a chair, flopping me across his lap like a rag doll. I sat curled up like a small child in the world's most splendid position, the cradle. He snuggled me close and the little girl inside was swept away. It was like being held by the Divine in flesh. I softly murmured, "This is what love must feel like."

To spend more time together, Tom and I joined the cast of a new play, *Beauty and the Beast*. We dated, danced, and acted, and I couldn't have been happier. On opening night, he announced that his parents had bought tickets for our first performance. Finally, I could meet the matriarch and patriarch of this Irish lad.

After the curtain dropped, Tom and I bolted toward the stage door in full makeup and costumes for this important greeting. I expected a genial hug, a familial kiss on the cheek, and an invite to the family picnic. Instead, I received eye-daggers. His mother and father stood in the lobby, arms crossed, puffs of smoke billowing out from all four ears. They hissed, "Hello," and turned their backs toward me, dragging their son into a nearby corridor for a private conversation. Their disapproval was palpable. I stood in the lobby, staggered.

Later that night, Tom explained that his parents were infuriated by our relationship, "My dad is pissed to the point of being explosive. He insists that I walk away from you and find a 'nice' girl with whom I can start a family. My mother told me I'd go down in the flames of Hell for dating a married woman with three kids. And, the Catholic Church would disown both of us."

I opened my mouth to stammer, "Huh? Flames of hell? Spontaneous combustion? The Church? Excuse me! I might be a bad singer and a late bloomer, but this is not *The Scarlet Letter*."

Tom's parental curse was a keen foreshadowing. We performed together over the next few weeks, but somehow, he was different. The adoring man I'd come to know became emotionally volatile, behaving like a neurotic little girl. He picked fights over inane things and pulled away, blaring in my face, "You don't understand me. You don't get it!"

I calmly offered Hoffman-like therapy, "Yes, I do understand. You're experiencing strong parental approval patterns, that's all." He couldn't hear my words.

One fateful day after our show closed, Tom invited me to his apartment. I stepped inside and stretched out my arms out for a welcoming embrace. Rather than showing me affection, he callously stepped away and abruptly announced, "I think we need to take a break."

My logical brain should have anticipated the blow, but my heart went into arrest. Overwhelmed with rejection, I moved to rage. "Break up with me?" I started screaming, and grabbed a special keepsake we'd purchased together, a hand-painted china cup that was sitting on his mantel. I ran outside to the front of his building for optimal viewing and dramatically raised my arm high over my head. I screamed at the top of my lungs and dashed the cup into a million pieces on the sidewalk. Several pedestrians scurried past in fear, as if I were a deranged inmate. It was like *The Jerry Springer Show* where distraught, betrayed females do crazy things for love. But there were no cameras here.

I'd found love for a brief four months and then it disappeared, lifted away in a gust of wind. My intellect rationalized our incompatibilities. Tom was ten years younger and without a college degree. He worked as a customer service telemarketer, had no career ambition, and wouldn't be a strong provider. My inner child, however, didn't care about our strategic misalignment. My emotional self wanted one thing: to curl up in Tom's lap forever.

My body shook with sobs as I tried to reach the bottom of the spear of anguish. This fatal heart-death left me grief-stricken. I cried so hard I couldn't breathe and I couldn't stop. Totally dysfunctional, I buried myself in my bedroom reading old love notes, listening to "I Will Always Love You." My eyes puffed out of their sockets.

The children approached me, worried about my well-being. "Are you okay, Mom?" For their sake, I made up stories about my newly acquired dust allergies, but I wasn't fine. I couldn't work and piles of tissues were growing across my room. My new golden heart had been flattened by the cleats of rejection. I wished I'd never ventured out on this ill-fated mission. I was destroyed.

In a desperate move, I called the Hoffman Institute and attended the graduate retreat that was scheduled for the following weekend. I flew off to California and coaxed some healing back into my broken psyche. I learned that Tom's rejection locked me into a childhood experience, a Dark Night. *Fire in the Soul*, a book written by fellow Hoffman grad Joan Borysenko, summarizes the chasm often created by childhood trauma.

> During a Dark Night our belief system is highly challenged and we are thrust into mortal combat with the forces of our own collective unconscious. For a variety of different reasons—loss, guilt, trauma, shame, war, shock—the world as we know it ceases to be

and we are left with no familiar ground to stand on. A period of inner chaos characterized by fear, doubt, terror, depression, or madness may follow.

—Joan Borysenko, *Fire in the Soul*

Tom's rejection spun me down a rabbit hole, a catastrophic Dark Night from when I was sixteen years old. My parents allowed me to have a good-bye sleepover party with my teenage girlfriends the night before we moved from Indianapolis to Chicago. These generous young ladies gave me a full-fledged tribute capturing the few years we'd spent together. They handed me gifts and promised to always be there. I listened to their supportive words, bursting spider veins under both eyes amid the tears.

Since I'd already moved five times, I couldn't fathom losing my new companions once again. As soon as the girls fell asleep, I walked mechanically into the bathroom, looking for drugs or razor blades, anything would do. I opened the cabinets searching for a way to kill myself. My mother, however, had already packed up the medicine chest, so my suicide attempt was thwarted.

Tom's abandonment dropped me back into the cyclone of childhood despair. I learned that my tears were not really for him, but rather for the sad little girl who couldn't sustain long-term meaningful relationships. My woe was really an unspoken desire to be loved unconditionally, accepted for who I am. Tom refused to do that. With a sense of tranquility, I returned to Chicago, solid and content once again.

❧ 12 ❧

Recession: The Great Equalizer

*I took a hard look at my materialistic choices. I'd naively
thought my financial abundance would continue forever;
I believed the economy would improve. My own desire for
possessions had led me to a terrifying financial cliff.*

∾

I put my recent experiences into the "grateful box,"
because after all, I'd taken an important first step
in discovering my heart. I also decided to stay close to
home for a while, turning my focus back toward being
a devoted mom and business executive. Our household
unit remained calm until the day Rob walked through
the front door on a Monday afternoon and announced,
"After five years, my entire department has been down-
sized and I only received two months of severance."

Rob pretended to be upbeat and assured me he would
launch his own entrepreneurial design business. But in a
stalling economy, that was going to be a tall order. I stared
at him in disbelief; a migraine drove across my right eye.
The family house was now on my shoulders. When I

originally manifested my dream home, times were wonderful, the country was strong, and I was married. Now, I had only one small marketing project, and soon there wouldn't be enough cash to pay for the money pit.

Rob and I were separated, but our finances were inextricably entwined with a mortgage, sizable equity loan, the kids' education, and now unemployment. To deliver a full confession, I'd also been siphoning off the equity loan to pay the primary mortgage. I knew it was a dangerous triage plan and prayed the bank wouldn't figure out I'd been paying off one loan with the other.

To make matters worse, the downsizing tattered Rob's ego. Day after day, he sat in his pajamas at the dining room surfing the Internet, applying to hundreds of online design opportunities, but to no avail. Then, one day out of the blue, he did something completely out of character. During a late-night infomercial binge, he purchased an eighteen-hundred-dollar instructional video detailing the process for reselling private loans. The following morning, he ran into the kitchen boasting of his accomplishment. "I purchased a kit that will teach me how to sell loans. It was expensive, but now I can make some money."

My blood boiled. "How could you do that? You don't have any financial loan experience. You're a total introvert and hate talking on the phone. You can't even get dressed!" Plain and simple, our debt avalanche was rolling straight down the hill toward our heads.

I fell for the whole American Dream: the cool house, sporty vehicle, latest version of electronics, and designer duds. These things are supposed to make you happy, right? Wrong. George Carlin said it best in 1980 when he proclaimed: "Your house is just a place to keep your stuff. If you didn't have so much stuff, you wouldn't need a house. In fact, your house is just a pile of stuff with a cover on it."

George nailed it. My big house was an ostentatious storage bin for lots of rubbish. The good news was I'd manifested a lot of "things," and my ability to create was strong. The bad news was I had no way to sustain my lifestyle and had inadvertently generated a financial abyss.

I'd fallen for the craze of retail consumption. Television advertising campaigns paint a sexy picture of what we need: smaller cell phones, designer iPad covers, sports cars, Chia Pets, and glitter nails. It's all fun for about a week, but then what? The new car gets a ding, there's a 10G space-age phone, and black nail polish is out of style. Be careful what you ask for; consumption can eat you alive.

The truth is all you really need is a toasty dry bed, some food, a nice-fitting outfit, a pair of comfortable shoes, and a spinning toothbrush. My essentials fit in a roller bag that goes under the seat in front of me.

We had a half-million-dollar primary mortgage, a growing fifty-thousand-dollar second mortgage, and a business loan weighing in at twenty-three thousand dollars. My lifestyle had become a fiendish pile of crap from which there was no way out.

Everyone knows you can't live off credit cards, because it creates a consuming debt that only increases over time. But when the grocery store clerk asked me, "How are you going to pay for that?" I looked him in the eye and handed him a Citigold with the looming limit. I was that cash poor.

Nearly penniless, I sat on my bed surrounded by bills, experiencing heart palpitations. The gas company wanted four hundred dollars for heat; karate class cost nine hundred dollars; rear Saab brakes were eight hundred bucks; the summer landscaper quoted twelve hundred to mow the lawn; and the vet told me the dog needed his teeth cleaned for three hundred smackers. By the way, when did it become necessary to anesthetize animals for tartar scraping?

Let's not forget about the insanity of owning a horse. I might as well have offered my arm, sliced it with a switch blade, and poured liquid green into a manure-filled stall for turnouts, blankets, shoes, and more nonsense than anyone could imagine.

I took a hard look at my materialistic choices. I'd naively thought my financial abundance would continue unabated; I believed the economy would forever soar. My own desire for possessions had led me to a terrifying financial cliff. Now, I had to stand for something new. I become the "Conservation Crusader." I took on a new form of existentialism, living ultra-lean. Rationally, I explained to the children, "The economy is down, Mom has no clients, Dad is out of work, and we need to cut down on everything.

"If we don't need it, we're not buying it. Sorry, kids, but we're canceling all private lessons and together we'll pitch in and take care of the yard. Buried deep down inside this house there's enough stuff to last us a lifetime and we're going to find it and use it up."

I also took the opportunity to add, "We're also planning a very special nonmonetary Christmas this year. Everyone will get one small gift under the tree and the rest will be thoughtful mementos that don't cost anything, like coupons for hugs, homemade brownies, back rubs, or a certificate for a chore-free day." I thought my ideas were clever, but I got three loud boos to the proposal. It simply didn't matter. I threw the dog a Milkbone for his teeth and coolly moved on with my speech, listing ways in which we would tighten our belts.

I reviewed my own consumptive habits first. As an iced-tea junkie, I kicked off the conservation movement by refusing to buy any more tea at coffee shops. It was much cheaper to make it at home. I scoured the cabinets, looking for a glass pitcher in preparation for my first brew and steep. There was no pitcher to be found. Therefore, in my new frugalness, I grabbed a large old glass flower vase. "This will work just fine," I hummed to myself.

When the kids got home from school, they opened the fridge and saw the container filled with a brown liquid. They asked, "Mom, what's with the vase in the fridge? Have you started gardening?"

I thought, *No, kids, your mom is just poor as dirt.* But instead of articulating my deep-seated worry for our financial future, I pulled out the flower pitcher and poured them each a glass.

I continued on my mission to cut expenses to the bone. We enjoyed macaroni and cheese several nights each week for $1.59 per box. I ate what was left on the spoon and that was fine with me. When I had a headache, I found myself on my knees looking under my bed for old dropped Tylenol tablets. *Why go to the store? There's got to be one here somewhere.* And, I lined our bathrooms with travel-sized hotel shampoos, conditioners, and body lotions that I had found in the basement. Plus, together we also rediscovered fun, free activities such as parks, bike rides, and cheap library videos.

Even if I couldn't spend money, I knew other people could. One afternoon I stopped by my parents' house to help Emma sell Girl Scout cookies to those who could afford them; grandparents always make the best customers. My father, ex-CEO, took this opportunity to corner me in the foyer. He gave me an unmistakable look, a penetrating stare as if he was going to confront me about my life choices.

These altercations were never pleasant, which is precisely why the entire family has my dad on a "Need to Know" status. He's like the colonel growling questions in the face of an innocent soldier. I have always tried to remain flanked by other family members to avoid such an attack or simply duck and run. But today, I had no such luck. *Oh God, here it comes!*

He began the confrontation. "So I heard from your mother that Rob is out of a job, you barely have any marketing projects, and the two of you are not really together. How exactly is that going to work?"

I immediately shot a .38-caliber "You are so dead" look straight at my mother while she sheepishly peered from around the corner. Just like a robber caught redhanded with the goods, I oozed with overwhelming desperation. I couldn't shove down the repressed mix of terror and misery any longer. I spontaneously ejected a guttural response, tears shooting horizontally from both eyes. "I don't know. I haven't slept in weeks. I am working as hard as I can. Rob got laid off. Things have never been right between us. I think we're going to have to move into your basement."

This vomit-like projection took my father off-guard. He hadn't seen me shed a tear in thirty years and just stood there stunned, looking around for instructions on how to properly behave in a highly emotive situation. Awkwardly, he patted my shoulder with the ends of his long fingers.

While I heaved uncontrollable sobs, my father moved to the far side of the room and paced back and forth, preparing his executive summary. "Okay, I got it. You are the sole provider, the mother, and primary caretaker. You can't do it alone."

I focused my eyes on the floor.

He paused again. "I'll tell you what I am prepared to do. I will loan you enough money on a month-to-month basis to pay the mortgage until you get out of this situation. But you will have to pay me back every cent. I place my bets on you."

I gulped, "Okay, thanks." I calmed down and started to breathe again for the first time in months. I didn't want to take a family loan, but desperate times call for desperate measures. This random act of kindness was a gift. I was falling into the eye of the repossession volcano and dragging my children along with me.

He gave me a handshake as I walked toward the door and told me he would write up a private loan document for me to sign, spoken like a true CEO. I handed him a carton of Thin Mints and left praying that someday I could pay forward the favor, perhaps leading my kids off a burning ledge when they need it the most.

～

SECTION V

Passionate Pursuits

～

⤖ 13 ⤖

Lessons from the Departed
(and Returned)

*I'd never before met anyone who'd died. So, I quickly rec-
ognized this as a unique opportunity to learn more about
the meaning of life from an authority, someone who'd
actually visited the "other side."*

∾

M y income anxiety attacks lessened as I used my
father's supplement to get us out of immediate
financial hot water and continued to practice financial
conservation. Right around that time, I received a random
email inviting me to attend a lecture by Mellen-Thomas
Benedict, a near-death-experience survivor. Benedict
had been pronounced dead for over an hour from a brain
tumor in 1982 and was now touring, holding a seminar
in a Unitarian church near my house. I'd never before
met anyone who'd died. So, I quickly recognized this as a
unique opportunity to learn more about the meaning of
life from an authority, someone who'd actually visited the
"other side."

According to Benedict, he had crossed over to heaven and was lifted into the "Light." There, he asked questions of his Guide for many hours before returning back to his lifeless body. He awoke with his nurse crying by his side and miraculously, his cancer was in complete remission.

> I remember waking up one morning at home around 4:30 AM, and I just knew that this was it. This was the day I was going to die. So I called a few friends and said goodbye. I woke up my hospice caretaker and told her. I had a private agreement with her that she would leave my dead body alone for six hours, since I had read that all kinds of interesting things happen when you die. I went back to sleep. The next thing I remember is the beginning of a typical near-death experience.
>
> —Mellen-Thomas Benedict, *Near-Death Experience (NDE) Story of Mellen-Thomas Benedict Journey Through the Light and Back*

Benedict stood before us at the neighborhood pulpit wearing a pallid gauze shirt, with an angelic glow surrounding him. He spoke to the large church audience about his heavenly conversation and addressed the fundamental insights revealed while being in a state of death.

> As I asked the Light to keep clearing for me, to keep explaining, I understood what the higher Self matrix is. We have a grid around the planet where all the higher Selves are connected. This is like a great company, a next

subtle level of energy around us, the spirit level, you might say. Then after a couple of minutes, I asked for more clarification. I really wanted to know what the universe is about, and I was ready to go at that time. I said, "I'm ready, take me." Then the Light turned into the most beautiful thing I have ever seen: a mandala of human souls on this planet.

—Mellen-Thomas Benedict, *Near-Death Experience (NDE) Story of Mellen-Thomas Benedict Journey Through the Light and Back*

In summary, Mellen-Thomas explained that we are all bound together in a web of connectivity, uniting us in a holographic cosmos. There is no beginning and no end, simply an ever-expanding now. There are only two aspects to life, "degeneration" and "generation." And, death is merely a shift from one state to another. Ultimately, there is no judgment in the Universe except during "Life Review," a critical part of the death process in which we experience exactly how we made others feel during our lives, the good and the bad.

Benedict also strongly reinforced the point that each of us are the "judge and the jury" of our own lives. Any personal redemption we hope to achieve comes from within, through self. "Remember this, and never forget it, you save, redeem, and heal yourself. You always have and you always will."

For over two hours, I listened intently to his tales. Although fascinating, they did not address the enormous question that's always on my mind: *Why are we here? What are we supposed to achieve?* For that reason, I did what you are not supposed to do during a lecture, interrupt.

Impulsively, I popped up from the Unitarian pew with my fingers raised high. The saintly man turned toward me, looking surprised.

I queried with a nervous squeak, "Since you've been beyond this Earthly plot, can you please tell me, what is our main objective? What are we supposed to accomplish while we're here?"

Benedict stood before me, our eyes locked. He languidly replied, "There is no real plan. We are creating the plan together. But in truth, we have come here to move to the next level of consciousness. That's all."

I knit my brow, puzzled. I'd expected an impressive formula, the one big "Ah-ha" from beyond. *What do you mean there's no real plan? I don't see people working together drafting a proposal for future universal happiness.* I shifted my weight from one foot to the other, refusing to sit down, continuing now on behalf of everyone at the event, "How do we do that? How do we find our higher consciousness? And how do we know when we're successful?"

The man in white smiled a holy grin. "Say everything that needs to be said; process all issues in your interpersonal relationships. Do your work here and love your life."

I didn't need to hear any more. I knew these were important ethereal concepts and slowly sat back down to record the pertinent points. With a surge of confidence, I snuck out the vestibule door and returned home to add four rules to "The Shortcuts for Living Well." These imperatives became my new strategic focus. I was committed to incorporating them into my life and pursuing my "higher consciousness," or so I thought.

Rule 11: Learn Your Lessons

Process your issues now. Learn your life lessons and work everything out in your interpersonal relationships.

Dianne's Initial Feedback

Although I've made some progress in learning lessons, I'm sure I still have a bumpy road ahead.

Rule 12: Speak Your Peace

Say everything that needs to be said. Always speak your truth in the moment.

Dianne's Initial Feedback

My tongue is a well-trained cover-up artist and I'm much better at saying what people want to hear rather than what's on my mind.

Rule 13: Live Your Authentic Self

The highest experience of love is the realization of what you believe in, who you are, and what you love to do. The only thing that's stopping you is you.

Dianne's Initial Feedback

I am totally committed to discovering my true desires and pursuing what I came here to do.

Rule 14: Love Your Life

Learn to love your life because you are the "dance." And in all aspects, pursue the wisdom of the heart.

Dianne's Initial Feedback

Love your life and follow your heart. This statement I completely understand.

❧ 14 ❧

Adventures in Online Dating

*I also met up with "Brutus," a bodybuilder who told me a
dumb joke and then smacked my bicep so hard, he bruised
it. I moved to escape, and the 230-pound guy "playfully"
pushed me into a wall. Terrified, I dashed to my car and
slammed down the lock. That was it: the sign to give up
dating forever.*

≈

Even though my outcome with Tom had been disas-
trous, I was ready to dive back into the dating pool.
This time, however, I chose a modern support tool: the
Internet. One lonely night while sitting in my office, I
uploaded two photos to the Match.com website, completed a witty profile, and wrote down my very simple
partnership criteria: nonsmoker who lived within twenty-
five miles, was at least five feet ten inches tall, and had
some education. I didn't want to be too picky. I hit the
"Upload File" button and closed my computer down for
the evening.

The next morning, I'd received forty "winks"
from interested males with gushing compliments and

provocative pitches. I was shocked at both the volume and how many men failed to meet my simple criteria. They were either too short, lived far away, or couldn't spell common English words. I hit "No, thanks" to all inquiries except one.

Greg was an educated business professional who worked for a suburban manufacturer. Based on his photograph, he looked like a regular hardworking Midwestern-type of guy. We shared a few pleasant email exchanges and I agreed to meet him at a north suburban pub.

I arrived early and scoped out a table near the door, just in case I needed to escape my first-ever blind date. Greg sauntered in wearing a navy wool blazer, white button-down shirt, brown loafers, and a beaming smile. I could tell he was uncomplicated and genuine.

Greg ordered us each a Harp Lager and told me humorous stories about his young children. His dry wit and comedic timing made me laugh to the point of crying; I liked him. Hanging out with this man was like trying on an old pair of slippers. While swapping tales about work and family, we uncovered a mutual affinity, adventure sports. Greg quickly took advantage of the discovery and invited me out for a second date, a skydiving trip to Ottawa, Illinois.

I've always been an adrenaline junkie. I get excited about Level V rapids, fast-moving cars, and daredevil roller coasters. And although terrified, ever since I was a little girl, I've been dying to jump out of a plane three thousand feet in the air. I knew it would be hard to find another forty-something who was willing to hurl themselves out of a moving aircraft, so I was delighted to accept his unique offer and cross this item off my midlife bucket list.

What can I say about skydiving? Getting into the hot fuchsia jumpsuit and the small crop plane was easy, especially because I had a small man hooked to my back. No, it wasn't Greg. Pete was my tandem instructor and lifeline. He was the petite fellow who taught me everything I needed to know and then tied himself to my shoulders and waist.

Pete and I crawled like a giant bug into the rear of the seatless crop duster and sat on the floor. Twenty other daredevils crawled in behind us. Greg and his instructor were miles away at the front of the craft, because the heavier the combined weight, the faster you fall. My date and his instructor jumped first and Pete and I were the last to go.

As other pairs launched, the man attached to my back seemed more like my *date* than *my* date. I was sitting on his lap as he scooted us forward, the whole time calling me "Sweetie."

While waiting to dive, a worrisome phenomenon developed: an oppositional battle between my multiple personalities. Part of me, the Crazy Driver, wanted to jump headfirst, fast and furious into the air. *This is awesome. Let's hurry up and feel the rush!* The other part of me, the Pragmatic Survivor, screamed, *Stop! Don't do it. It might be your last day alive.* Pleas from the Pragmatic Survivor escalated until a sense of panic overwhelmed me; I felt weak and sick. *I guess I'm just a big chicken after all!* I swung my head around to see Pete's face and claimed, "I changed my mind. I don't want to jump. I'll just land with the plane."

The man behind me had other ideas. He smirked, the sunlight glimmering across his straight teeth. "Keep moving, Sweetie. We're next, even if I have to shove your pink bottom out of here." He was a tough-love kind of guy.

Through my gut-wrenching dread, Pete pushed me inch by inch toward the tiny checkerboard farmland below.

When we reached the door, he blared in my ear, "Trust me. Lean your head back on my shoulder, close your eyes, and I will jump for both of us." In that moment, I leaned my head backward and accepted my potential death.

The free fall was bitterly cold, with my cheeks flapping wildly. As we harshly cut through ten thousand feet of air, I found the free fall both distressing and exhilarating at the same time. It was like battling a formidable foe, Mother Earth, to maintain position and balance. It was the ultimate contest to determine who would win: me or the hard ground below. Yet, at the designated altitude, I gracefully reached behind onto Pete's hip, pulled the knob, and our chute exploded upward. The gentle glide toward planet terra was soft and serene.

This leap was more than just a thrill-seeking dive; it was a metaphor for life transformation. Every time I had to make a big shift, I felt frightened, secretly wanting to turn back. But with a large dose of courage and sometimes a shove from behind, I leapt forward and managed to maneuver through the free fall. The first part of the journey was painful, fighting to establish a solid position in space, but the final float was a stupendous natural "high."

With this sage insight, I gave myself long overdue kudos for turning around a life that had been charging off course. I was tremendously thankful for having the opportunity to reinvent myself and actively pursue adventure with a wide-open heart. And while drifting in the air, I honestly reflected upon my dating prospects: I didn't have romantic chemistry with Greg, or with Pete for that matter, but it certainly was a memorable day.

After jumping into the cosmos with Greg, I continued to explore a flow of unforgettable online dates.

Journal Entry

Over the past few months, I've ventured out on count-less Match.com dates and my baggage cart is now officially full of abysmal experiences. The Internet has impaired my most fundamental matchmaking ability: judgment. Anyone can upload a picture and type a message on a keyboard, but without using my eyes, ears, and other primary senses to screen initial data, I'm handicapped. Online photos and pithy pro-files are smoke screens used to hide scars, spasms, strange growths, uni-brows, and even insane behav-ior. Online dating has not only wasted my time, but gallons of gasoline. Therefore, I've affectionately re-named the service "Dysfunctional.com" to accurately reflect my encounters.

On my last Internet date, I arrived at the restaurant excited to meet a seemingly "attractive" prospect named Tim. I could immediately tell the man was shorter and heavier than his e-channel photo. *Here we go again.* I spent time to get dressed, carefully apply makeup, and battle rush-hour traffic to eat a meal with a stranger whose scalp was covered with sore red hair plugs.

To top it off, when I started to describe my marketing business, Tim rolled his excruciatingly long tongue slowly out of his mouth until it reached full length, like a cat stretching after a nap. He then kept it protruded out for the longest thirty seconds of my life. I looked behind me, searching for someone, anyone who was also beholding this frightening display. Sorry to say, no one else in the restaurant was paying attention. Then, just as bizarrely as he pulled it out, this utterly strange man slowly curled the appendage back inside. Wonderful! I had the good fortune of viewing another inventive dating tic. At the end of our painful meal, Tim leaned forward to give me a sloppy kiss. No, thanks! There's no telling where that tongue-of-a-frog has been.

The Internet also seemed to ignite male hunting behavior. Why date a lone mare when you can score the herd? A nice-looking Internet prospect named John took me out for sushi. While biting into a tasty salmon-skin hand roll, John mentioned that he was thoroughly enjoying his recent separation. On Mondays and Wednesdays he was engaged in regular "relations" with a lovely lady named Tami. He added, "Tami's a cute, nice girl who has me targeted for future marriage material." With soy sauce dripping from his chin, John then shared the specifics of his relationship with Sue, a striking bombshell he'd reserved for Thursday nights. Neither of these women knew John was a dog. Exhausted but not quite satiated, my date had the nerve to ask, "Hey, Dianne, do you want to go out with me on Saturday?" There was only one response to that nasty proposition: "Over my dead body!"

After witnessing the feline behavior of Tim and the canine nature of John, Internet dating got worse. I went dancing with a surgeon who showed up looking like Richard Simmons, with a sweatband around his tight greased curls and black spandex pants. He waved jazz hands at me all night and I could barely control my laughter. I also met up with "Brutus," a bodybuilder who told me a dumb joke and then smacked my bicep so hard, he bruised it. I moved to escape, and the 230-pound guy "playfully" pushed me into a wall. Terrified, I dashed to my car and slammed down the lock. That was it: the sign to give up dating forever.

ᗯ 15 ᗗ

Passion and Addiction

On one hand, Jeff was intelligent, entertaining, and ador-
ably cute. And, on the other hand, he was a recovering
alcoholic who was living with his mother and didn't have a
driver's license. My Pragmatic Survivor yelled, "He's not
a dating prospect. Dianne, walk away!"

ᗕ

Just when I was about to hit the "Cancel Membership"
button on my Match account, I received a "wink" from
an intriguing man named Jeff, who held master's degrees
in both mechanical engineering and business. Jeff's photo
featured a tall, tan, muscular man driving a powerboat,
wind blowing through his full head of sandy hair. I love
boats! According to Jeff's profile, he was a divorced engineering corporate vice president and father of three lively
little girls. *He's really good-looking. Okay. I'll talk to him.*

During our first call, Jeff was bright, quirky, and self-
deprecatingly funny. He also seemed more than willing
to openly shared the details of his downsized adulthood.
According to Jeff, his ex-wife called off their marriage, put

their suburban house on the market, and hit him on the head with a golf club all in the same week. Recently, he'd memorialized his fortieth birthday by piercing his left earlobe and inking three colorful tattoos across his back, one for each daughter. Oh, and by the way, he was living with his mother to recover financially, post-divorce.

Personally, I am not into piercings, tattoos, or guys who cohabitate with mommy, but my household arrangement was less than traditional, so I reminded myself once again not to judge.

As our conversation drew to a close, Jeff added, "You probably won't want to date me because I live an hour north of you, but I'd love to buy you a cup of coffee. I'm starting a new engineering business and I'll need some help with my marketing materials in the future. Will you look at my biography and give me some feedback?"

I really didn't want to meet this man because I knew there had to be some reason why his ex-wife had hit him in the head with a four-iron. But, I was still cash poor and in search of the almighty dollar, so I countered, "My riding stable isn't far from your neighborhood. The next time I'm in your area, we can get together to talk about business. I do need to warn you, however, I might be wearing breeches."

The following week I met Jeff at the only coffee place in his neighborhood, a Starbucks tucked inside a local grocery store. He sauntered in wearing a plaid flannel shirt, khaki army coat, and hiking boots, looking more like a lumberjack than a business professional. He extended his hand and softly called my name. My jaw hit the table. Unlike my other Internet companions, Jeff was bronzed, chiseled, and positively the most attractive man I'd ever met.

He was gentle, sensitive, and smart, in a gawky sort of way. I kept our conversation professional and dutifully reviewed his engineering bio, making lots of edits. When I stood up to leave, Jeff grabbed me for an affable bear hug. Caught off guard by his touch, I clumsily stood frozen, my cheeks blushing with heat. I could tell he was smitten.

In addition to multiple academic degrees, Jeff held a Ph.D. in rolling strings of honey-like sweetness from his tongue. He called me later that evening and littered the phone line with compliments regarding my intellect, compassion, humor, riding pants, and figure. Then he launched into a soliloquy. "I have to come clean. I am a recovering alcoholic and have been sober for five years. And I volunteer to help others battle the disease. Here's the kicker: six months ago I lost my driver's license when my car had mechanical failure and I accidently hit a tree. After my court date, everything will return to normal. I think you're an amazing woman and I'd like to see you again."

It was a lot to take in. On one hand, Jeff was intelligent, entertaining, and adorably cute. But on the other hand, he was a recovering alcoholic living with his mother and didn't have a driver's license. My Pragmatic Survivor yelled: "He's not a dating prospect. Dianne, walk away!"

Did I take heed? No, I did not. What can I say? I was bored, lonesome, and had no other weekend plans, so I drove up to meet Jeff as a "friend" to hear a band play at the historic Mineola Hotel on the banks of Fox Lake. He stood close, swaying back and forth. Every time I spoke, Jeff interrupted, articulating minute observations: "You have gold speckles in the shape of a star in the center of your eyes." "Your hair breaks into banana curls after you perspire." "You must have been Renoir's model for his paintings in the Louvre."

We danced to the hits of the eighties, laughing, smiling, and sweaty until the lights turned on. On our way out to the car, Jeff wrapped his warm coat around me to make sure I was extra comfortable in the cool night air. He pulled me toward him and while tucking me in the cocoon of his vestment, snuck in a luxuriously slow, gentle kiss. I protested, "Wait! We're just friends."

He wrapped me even tighter in two powerful arms. I melted. *This guy is good!* I thought to myself. I managed to twist away and scoot inside my vehicle for a long drive home, but I couldn't stop thinking about the charged kiss that lingered on my lips.

Over the next few weeks, I buried myself in auditioning, work, and kids while Jeff barraged me with emails, text messages, and phone calls. One Saturday afternoon while driving out to the barn, he called and requested, "My little girls have been cooped up at my house all day and need to get outside. Since you are coming up here anyway, can I bring them to your barn to meet the horse? I promise we won't stay long."

It all seemed quite innocent, so I agreed.

Sharon, Jeff's mother, drove the entourage out to the stable in a clanking old Cadillac. Charred cigarette butts flew out from the driver's door as she exited to greet me. Sharon wheezed a pleasant "Hello" and grabbed my hand for a hearty welcome. I couldn't help but notice her large frame, unstable gait, and sallow skin. In contrast, three adorably precocious blond girls popped out of the car filled with vim and vigor, racing to meet Rose, my trusty mare.

That afternoon, Jeff managed his mother's short abusive insults like a gentleman as I marched each child around for an extensively long pony ride on the Thoroughbred's back. Everyone had a terrific time. Jeff offered to stay and help me put away the saddle and brush the animal while Sharon drove the girls back home. I picked the horse's hooves while he excused himself and walked out of the barn to take a personal call.

When he returned, Jeff's hazel eyes were misty. "I just received notice that my ex-wife is taking me to court and fighting for supervised visitation. She is a bitter, power-hungry witch with the money and connections to take my children away from me. I'll just die."

I stood there watching this charming man break down and my heart ached. I reached out to give him a comforting embrace. Jeff must have sensed my empathy and secret pangs of attraction. He must have known my body missed being cradled. He dried his eyes and swept me up in his arms, lifting me high off the floor with a sigh. "You are so important to me. Will you go out with me next weekend?" His body felt so delicious, I gave in.

Everything about him seemed too good to be true. I met Jeff downtown for Italian cuisine and a cabaret show and he lavished me with unwavering attention, commenting, "You really don't need to wear any makeup; you're the most stunning woman I ever met. Don't move; stop right there so I can capture your beauty on film." Who says these things to a middle-aged woman with crow's feet and means it? He lifted his phone to take a photograph. Quite frankly, it was refreshing to experience an evening out without experiencing any weird tics, being shoved, or even a drop of alcohol.

Jeff's passion was enchanting and after my experience with Tom, endless doting was just what the doctor ordered. I became hooked on this man's love and his touch. We quickly started dating and saw each other as often as possible, experiencing a sublimely affectionate two-month-long honeymoon phase. Once again, my heart was soaring.

Everything was perfect in our relationship until the night Jeff called me and begged, "I need you to drive me to an appointment tomorrow. I have to meet with my probation officer. My mother has to go the doctor and can't take me. If I don't go, I'll be in violation of a court order and they'll put me in jail. Can you PLEASE drive me?"

"What are you talking about?" I fired back. "I knew you had to go to court for an accident, but you never mentioned probation! Why do you have a probation officer?"

Apologetically, Jeff divulged the truth. Apparently, in January, he drove his car into a tree, but it wasn't due to mechanical failure. Jeff received a DUI from the county sheriff and was on full probation due to a prior DUI conviction six years earlier. He pleaded frantically, "I'm sorry. I should have told you, but I love you so much and I'm terrified you'll leave me. Stay with me through this difficult period and we can put it all behind us."

My head was spinning. *He told me he'd been sober for many years. Why didn't he tell me about the DUIs? Did he just say he loved me?*

I felt a sharp boring sensation in the base of my gut like a spinning power tool. Hicks would have called this a "fuzz buster warning"; she would've advised me to immediately change my course toward something more positive. Bells and whistles were going off and my intuition was screaming, but I was already too deeply in love with Jeff to do anything but choose my heart. I canceled an important business meeting and agreed to be his chauffeur.

The following day, I drove Jeff to the probation office, right between the Gurnee courthouse and the Gurnee jail. I couldn't help but notice the cast of characters seated inside. One guy was wearing a baggy tank top with low-riding pants and red plaid boxers flooding over the top. Another man looked like a modern gangster in a head-to-toe white suit, black sunglasses, and slick black hair. A third man was slumped in the corner, his scraggly gray beard propped up against the wall. The place gave me the creeps. I took a seat in the corner while Jeff registered with the receptionist, who sat behind bullet-proof glass. Feeling very uncomfortable, I pushed my sunglasses high up on my nose and covered my face with a *National Geographic*. I pretended to be invisible.

A short African-American man in a crisp white shirt and fire-engine red tie stepped through the guarded metal archway. He looked at me curiously and inquired as to my identity. Jeff popped up, emptied his pockets onto my lap, grasped the man's hand, and enthusiastically introduced me as his "girlfriend."

The two men passed through the metal detector, and five minutes later, Jeff stormed back through, grinding his teeth and grunting like a caveman, "Let's get out of here!" He raced out of the building and I followed. While driving to Jeff's house, he explained that the probation officer had made sexually offensive remarks about me in their meeting. Demonstrating a complete lack of self-control, Jeff had become irate and refused to take the required Breathalyzer test. He stormed out of the office and the rest was history.

I shrieked, "You did what? Who cares about what he said? Your court date is in two weeks."

Jeff nervously called his lawyer to report the incident and the attorney insisted that he schedule a new meeting to smooth out the "misunderstanding." As fate would have it, the officer left the next day on a vacation and the only available appointment time was right before Jeff's DUI trial.

My boyfriend turned toward me, eyes darting in fear. Sick bubbles foamed, growing inside my throat. I wanted to run screaming. One minute, I was in a deliriously amorous relationship with a hunk and the next gravely concerned that my boyfriend might get locked up.

Over the years, I'd had a couple of parking tickets, but I'd always paid them on time. This was unfamiliar territory. As a responsible person, I reviewed my participation in the drama. *I knew something felt wrong when I entered the probation office and I should have stayed in the car. I'm partly to blame here.*

On the afternoon of his hearing, I drove Jeff back to meet with his probation officer. Once again, fate played a role. The man had been detained in another pressing court case and rescheduled Jeff's meeting; the next time Jeff would see him was in front of a judge. In a total panic, the two of us ran down prisoner's row to find the lawyer.

Jeff's case was swiftly called to the bench. The wizened magistrate read the file in silence, a gnarled finger underlining every word. After only a few minutes, he stiffly turned toward the accused, "Mr. Barker, did you refuse to take the Breathalyzer test during your last probation visit?"

The attorney interrupted, gesturing toward the probation officer who was standing erect next to the bench. "Your Honor, my client tried to reschedule the probation meeting but his contact was on vacation. He also canceled Mr. Barker's appointment prior to this hearing."

The judge ignored him. "Based on the lack of cooperation, I can only assume you were drinking. Since this is your second DUI, your probation will be extended for three more months. You'll need to spend five hundred hours in an in-treatment alcohol recovery program and right now, you're going to jail. We'll take a blood sample while you're in there to make sure there's no alcohol in your system and I'm posting a twenty-five-thousand-dollar bail so you're not tempted to leave the area. Do you understand the situation?"

Jeff whimpered, "Yes, Your Honor."

A policeman threw Jeff's arms behind his back and cuffed him. Jeff looked back toward me, his face white with fright. There was no talking, no coordinating, and no good-byes. I sat there stunned, helpless, having witnessed a brutal injustice. *This was a hideous mistake! My boyfriend was escorted to jail and I'd never seen the man drink.* I felt so sick I ran into the ladies' room and threw up.

Jeff's lawyer paced agitatedly back and forth in the hallway and upon my return rattled off a plan for the next hearing date. He handed me his card.

I choked, "What do I do now?"

The man explained, "Come back to the jailhouse with two thousand five hundred dollars in cash, which is ten percent of the bond needed to get him out. He'll crack up if he stays in there too long."

I obeyed. With the sun sinking in the sky, I peeled out of the parking lot and drove around the unfamiliar suburb frantically looking for a Citibank branch. Pulsing red and blue lights swirled behind my car. My heart almost beat out of my chest. *Am I a fugitive? Does every policeman know I just came from the courthouse? Am I going to jail too?* My whole body quivered.

"You turned right at a no-right-turn-on-red intersection," stated the unforgiving man in a navy uniform and bulletproof vest.

I wanted to spill my guts and confess my filthy secret; I wanted to tell him I was trying to make bail. But instead, I was terrified that he'd think I was part of a criminal sect, so I knit my lips tightly together. The police officer studied my shaking hands and eyes, white with fear and then sternly handed me a one-hundred-fifty-dollar ticket, walking away with my license. *Could this day get any worse?*

It took me more than an hour to find a bank, but eventually I returned to the ominous penitentiary with a wad of cash. An armed guard met me at the door. After all, this is where criminals stay. I handed the bailiff a lump of hundreds and she gave me a handwritten receipt for human liberation announcing, "It's the prisoners' dinnertime. You just missed the last release of the day. You can pick up your party tomorrow morning at seven."

I felt as if she had punched me in the gut. I glanced at the clock. It was five fifteen and my boyfriend was going to spend the night in jail because I couldn't get the money fast enough. *This time, it was certainly my fault.*

I drove home that evening excruciatingly slowly, taking side roads to avoid more trouble with the law. When I returned, I gave each one of my kids an intensely long embrace and silently thanked the Universe for keeping them safe. Then, I crawled deep inside my closet and made a private phone call that couldn't be overheard. I dialed Sharon. She gasped when I explained the day's events. "This is terrible! It will send him over the edge!"

"What do you mean by that?" I probed.

"When things go wrong, Jeff can't handle adversity and sometimes slips back into a dark place. He could even start drinking again." I didn't completely understand the "dark place" reference, but Sharon agreed to pick up her son from prison the following morning.

After the children went to bed, I paced back and forth, processing the intense stress. I called Catherine, a truly genuine and reasonable girlfriend, to empty my guilty coffers. Catherine listened in silence for a long time, but I could feel tension building across the line. When I finished my story, she exploded with monumental concern, "You're dating a drunk. You have to get out of this relationship. You are a sane, rational woman and everything you told me is crazy talk."

I rushed to Jeff's defense. "But I was there. I saw what happened. This man was a victim of the court system, not a criminal."

My friend got louder. "Dianne, things like this don't just happen. I've dated alcoholics and they lie incessantly. He didn't take the Breathalyzer test because he was drinking the day he was supposed to see his probation officer. He's incapable of telling you the truth."

Indignant, I shot back, "Don't worry! I won't ever talk to you about any of my relationships again." I slammed the phone down. *Why did she say these things to me?*

When Jeff returned home, he told me he had to walk in circles around the holding cell all night with ten other shoeless prisoners to stay warm because the room was freezing and footwear was prohibited. He implored, "I didn't deserve this! I'm doing everything right and getting my life back on track. I adore you and I'm sorry you had to witness such a horrendous scene. Please don't leave me."

I reassured him, "I love you too." I wasn't going anywhere. I knew I was breaking every rule for *Living Well*. I was not feeling positive, staying in alignment, or minding my own matters. Instead, I had become addicted to Jeff's copious adoration and completely one with the horrific mess.

Shedding light on the topic, a book by Gregg Braden, *The Divine Matrix*, explains that in the face of conflict, disease, war, or intense emotions, over time we've all been conditioned to give a piece of ourselves away.

> For every piece of ourselves that we've given away to be where we are in life today, there's an emptiness that's left behind, waiting to be filled. We're constantly searching for whatever it is that fills our particular void. When we find someone who has the very things we've given away, it feels good to be near him or her. The person's complementary essence fills our inner void and makes us feel whole again. . . . When we find our "missing" pieces in others, we'll be powerfully and irresistibly drawn to them. We may even believe that we "need" them in our lives, until we remember that we're so attracted to in them is something that we still have within us . . . it's simply sleeping.
>
> —Gregg Braden, *The Divine Matrix*

Over the following week, Jeff fell into a cavernous depression. He sat slumped inside his mother's home, refusing to call clients or discuss his required in-patient recovery program. As I watched him with pity and distress, a new part of my personality emerged: The Rescuer. Instead of following Braden's advice and giving myself the "missing pieces" of my essence—space, care, and support—I threw on my crisp nurse's uniform and made it my job to save Jeff from his own life.

I researched every in-patient recovery program in the area, including regional centers, hospitals, and state facilities. After begging, borrowing, and pleading, I secured an opening for him at a site located on the north side of Chicago.

Jeff sat quietly inside my car during our long ride to the rehab center, making circles with his finger on the inside of the frosty glass. I pulled up in front of the tan brownstone building, but the man refused to get out. I pressed, "Please, just follow the program for three weeks and then we can put it all behind us. Think of it as a vacation of sorts." After an uncomfortably long delay, Jeff shoved the car door open hard and stumbled unsteadily down the icy walkway and I scooted behind.

The program administrator took Jeff's bag for inspection and handed him the all too familiar Breathalyzer. Jeff smirked, squinted, and blew hard. The administrator held the machine high over his head to display the results. Jeff's blood alcohol level was twice the legal limit.

I hollered, "What? Did you drink this morning before I picked you up?"

Oh, yes, he had. Jeff had officially relapsed.

The administrator's voice changed from friendly to serious. "Mr. Barker, you'll need to go into our detoxification unit for several days before we can admit you to the program. This will add time and cost to your treatment. However, you're very lucky because we have one bed available."

While the man completed the additional paperwork, Jeff sat slumped in a chair and I stood erect, with fists clenched. I wanted to hit him on the head and probably would have, if there had been a golf club handy. The administrator handed me a card with "Family Day" circled in red. "We need to see you here in two weeks for a group visit and private meeting."

In a fury I retorted, "I'm just the chauffeur and girl-friend. I'm sure Jeff's mom will attend the family meeting."

The man touched my arm lightly, insisting, "You need to come!" and escorted Jeff to his detox bedroom.

I drove home feeling utterly betrayed, wheels spinning wildly in the snow. I had worked hard to get Jeff in a program before his next court date. *Why did he choose today to drink? Was he trying to get kicked out?* Cruising down the street in a mental fog, I nearly missed the entrance to my white-etched street. I swung the steering wheel to the left and the car started to skid. Bam! I hit the curb. I pulled into my driveway with a ripped tire and bent rims.

The Universe speaks to us in many ways. Getting tickets, twisted ankles, and having accidents are deliberate messages, wake-up calls. These unexpected troubles indicate that we're not grounded and must regroup. Since Jeff had actually relapsed, it would have been best for me to end our relationship and allow him to focus on his recovery. But as Family Day approached, I sat in my big comfy house, pinched with guilt about the probation officer, the overnight in jail, and the rehab lockup. When Sharon told me she wasn't planning to attend the "special" day with her son, culpability squeezed even harder around my waist. I didn't want to go back to the facility, but I did anyway.

On Family Day, visitors took their seats in a meeting room that looked like a seventies frat house, with frayed orange couches and ripped lemon-tangerine-striped wall-paper. The patients marched in: a grungy young teenager, a pregnant Goth girl, several unkempt young adults, and a clean-cut man in a polo shirt. Jeff sauntered in, tall, relaxed, and smiling from ear to ear. He looked innocent as he sat down on the couch next to me and sweetly took my hand. His eyes beamed with adoration; he was delighted to see me. I breathed a long sigh of relief, knowing that he was well.

During my visit, I attended several lectures regarding addictive personalities and the well-meaning loved ones who often try to save the addict from their own actions. Recovering alcoholics struggle every day with not drinking, and unless they actively participate in a recovery program like Alcoholics Anonymous, typically they relapse under stress. Lying, concealing information, and creating drama are standard addiction coping mechanisms.

According to Dr. Charles Whitfield, author of *Healing the Child Within*, "Co-dependence is one of the most common conditions causing confusion and suffering in the world."

> Co-dependence is a condition that stifles our True Self, our Child Within . . . We can begin to define co-dependence as any suffering and/ or dysfunction that is associated with or results from focusing on the needs and behavior of others. Co-dependents become so focused upon or preoccupied with important people in their lives that they neglect their True Self.
>
> —Charles L. Whitfield, M.D.,
> *Healing the Child Within*

I was definitely neglecting my True Self and totally preoccupied with Jeff and his problems, yet, I was still completely blind. *How did all this co-dependence information apply to me?* Jeff completed his in-treatment program and returned home, extra caring and sensual in our relationship. He also attended regular AA meetings and worked diligently to get his business back on track. Tranquility, unfortunately, never lasted long in this man's world.

One evening Jeff called me hysterically, "I missed the train to your house because my mother came into my room and stole my wallet and keys when I was in the shower. She's crazy! Sharon's threatening to call the police if I try to pry my stuff out of her hands. If she calls, it will go on my probation record. I don't have any other way to get cash. Can you drive up here and get me?"

The situation was certifiably insane, but what choice did I have? It took me an hour and a half in traffic, but I pulled up to Jeff's house with the lights ablaze. He stormed out, swinging a packed suitcase and waving his recently released wallet in his hand. We drove off and agreed it was time for him to rent his own space. I offered to let him stay in my office loft and sleep on a cot until he found a suitable apartment. Jeff threw his strapping muscular arms around me and we celebrated a new beginning.

It was enchanting to have him close by and a delightful reprieve from the previous month's events. Within a week, Jeff located a cozy apartment in Winnetka with full amenities and asked the management company to prepare the lease.

On the morning of his move, I stopped by my office to pick up Jeff and his belongings. I turned the key in my sturdy office door, but the wood banged hard against the metal chain. It was locked from the inside. I pushed it open a few inches and peered through the narrow crack; there was Jeff's body sprawled across on the floor. I shouted his name but he didn't move.

Panicked, I drove wildly back to my house and grabbed a pair of wire cutters from the garage. I returned and snapped the chain off from the outside with brute force. As it fell to the ground, I rushed over to Jeff, who was lying there in his shorts, his nose, hands and legs splattered in blood. He was snoring loudly. The white carpet underneath him was stained reddish brown and food wrappers were everywhere. I stood up to assess the situation, peered into the bathroom, and there I found vomit and chunks of green beer-bottle glass on the floor. Someone obviously had a wild night of partying.

I commanded, "Get up! What's the matter with you? Have you been drinking? How could you relapse after all we have been through?"

I grabbed a towel and examined the wound on his leg. Jeff woke from his stupor and tried to kiss me. I shoved him down. "Were you drinking?" I demanded an answer.

He murmured, "I only had one beer. I must have fallen in the bathroom and hit my nose and knee on the floor, but I'm fine. Don't worry."

Like an FBI agent, I scoured the office hunting for evidence, opening every drawer and cabinet. There it was: a grocery bag filled with empty Heineken bottles hidden in the back of the closet. "You lied to me," I hissed. I threw his suitcase at him. "Get out of here. Get out of my life. We're done!"

Jeff snapped, "Forget you. Who needs you anyway? You're an ugly bitch!"

Jeff stormed out and I knelt down weeping as I scrubbed up his puke and blood. *I thought he loved me. How could he do this to us?*

I refused to speak to Jeff until he sorted himself out. He moved into his new apartment but continued to hound me with text messages and emails. Like a professional stalker, he stood outside my office and knocked softly on the door, whispering, "I miss you so much. I made a huge mistake. I'm sorry."

I wanted to remain strong, but I was emotionally entwined and psychologically hooked to the yo-yo strings of our relationship. Also at my age, I was petrified I'd never again find such all-encompassing attraction and adoration. *No one has ever cared for me so deeply. I don't want to be alone night after night for the rest of my life.* I let hope rule my world. *I know he can change if he wants to.*

Softened, I took Jeff back and this time, I set boundaries. "It's a new beginning for us. Promise me you'll remain sober from this day forward. Swear to God that you'll never touch liquor again." Jeff gave me his solemn oath.

A month passed, but as usual, Jeff's life was dotted with unfavorable events. One day he called me hysterically. "My wife found out about my overnight in jail and just won the petition for supervised custody. Sharon has to be present during all visits with my kids."

I did my best to console him, but this poor man was crushed. Jeff holed up in his new apartment and wouldn't answer the phone. I stopped by the following evening with a plate of cookies to cheer him up. The door was unlocked, so I cautiously turned the brass knob. As it opened, I gagged, hit with a wall of overpowering stench. Jeff was lying facedown naked on the mattress, his hips surrounded by a pool of feces and urine. An empty fifth of tequila sat squarely on the kitchen counter. He must have finished the whole thing, worm and all. That bottle contained enough alcohol to kill a person.

I stood motionless, trying to decide whether or not to call 911, when Jeff woke from his stupor. He lifted his head and nailed me with a deadly stare, violently snarling, "What are you doing here?" He looked like a gruesome monster, possessed. I was so frightened by his evil demeanor, I dropped the plate of cookies and swung around to leave. Jeff lifted his body covered with brown poop and grabbed my sleeve, trying to hurl me to the floor. I screamed, twisted in the opposite direction, and pried my coat out of his clumsy grasp. I sprinted all the way to the car, knowing I'd just narrowly escaped an assault. When I got home, I locked myself in the bedroom, wrapped my arms around my knees, and rocked convulsively for hours.

Strangely, that night I received an eerie voicemail from Mel Doerr, one of my favorite Chicago psychics. He stated, "I had a scary dream about you last night and I don't usually dream about my clients. You need to come see me." I gasped.

Mel is well-known in the Midwest, and the Chicago police often use his services to help provide information for unsolved crimes. In fact, in a regional television interview, Mel accurately predicted the circumstances surrounding Natalee Holloway's internationally known 2005 disappearance, years prior to Joran van der Sloot's confession.

Typically I'd visit Mel at the beginning of each year to get a sense of the months to come. He'd always been dynamic, colorful, and incredibly accurate. He called me "Blanche," a strange but entertaining pet name. Upon entering Mel's smoky office covered with pictures of wolves, his face was serious and drawn. "Someone is trying to hurt you, Blanche. I dreamt that you were hanging out with a fiend. What is going on?"

My horror story gushed forth. It was a relief to openly share the full tale of Jeff's tormented world with a supportive individual. Mel grabbed an antique blue fountain pen and began drawing frantically. He presented me with an image of a man in a jail surrounded by police cars. "You're in danger. He will hurt you in many ways if you continue with him. You have to end this relationship and never see him again. It's not only for your safety, but for that of your children."

That was it. It was as if Mel snapped his fingers in my face and I woke up from the trance. What started as a journey to find my heart had become pure lunacy. This man's life was filled with travesties: substance abuse, addiction, lies, jail, and now violence. Catherine tried to tell me, but I wouldn't listen. I had accidents, tickets, and warnings, all of which I ignored. *How could I have put myself and the children in danger? This was not how I was supposed to be living.*

Jeff recovered from his near–alcohol poisoning and tried to rekindle our relationship, but I was done. I spoke with complete candor, "Jeff, I care for you, but I finally figured out what's wrong."

"What's that?" he carefully queried.

I continued my monologue, "I finally realized that you don't want to be here. I wake up every day and work hard to create a nice life for myself and the kids. You almost killed yourself the other night because you can't take the punches the world has to offer. Clearly, you want to die, so I recommend that you stop torturing all the women who love you like your mother, your daughters, and me. Maybe it'd be best if you just 'passed over.'" I added, "Based on what I saw the other night, I agree with your ex-wife. You need supervised visitation with your children."

Jeff gulped. "Are you telling me to kill myself?"

With fortitude I retorted, "I think you've been trying to kill yourself for a long time and alcohol is just your weapon of choice." I added, "I can't watch you destroy your life and I won't let you destroy mine. Don't ever contact me again."

My words didn't actually stop him. A few days later, Jeff walked to the front of my house at midnight and rang the bell. The ringing sent our angry terrier barking madly, but I refused to answer. I peeked out of the second-floor window and halted in fear as I watched Jeff's tall, lanky body slowly retreating into the shadowy darkness.

The next morning, I called Sharon to deliver an imposing warning, "I'll file a restraining order if your son ever calls or stops by my home or office again." She begged me not to initiate more trouble with the law and somehow she made him stop.

Journal Entry

I found a state of unconditional embrace with Jeff, a romantic, all-encompassing obsession. He enveloped me with his body and mind; accepting my imperfections and craving me anyway. I was terrified to let him go because I knew the intensity of our union would be impossible to replace. I warned countless times, "If you drink again, I won't stay." I've agonized, watching the man I love self-destruct, but the disease was far more powerful than my words. Alcohol has utterly possessed this man's soul.

To soothe my broken heart, I read *Breaking Free from the Victim Trap* by Diane Zimberoff. Within its pages, the book brilliantly details the foundation of all dysfunctional relationships, the "Hero-Victim-Villain Triangle." This cycle especially applies to those involved with addictive personalities. The book shows how to return to health by refusing to play any of the following roles: "hero," "victim," or "villain." It explains the importance of taking full responsibility for our own lives and for holding others accountable for running their own.

> The victim triangle is a true picture of how unclear the boundaries can get within the victim relationship. The people constantly go back and forth between the different roles with lightning speed. The boundaries between each individual person are so foggy that a clear sense of identity is difficult. . . . Also, because so much guilt is used to control, the individual members do not know what they really want. The individuals are so involved in the family games and cover-ups that clear independent individuality are not present.
>
> —Diane Zimberoff, *Breaking Free*
> *from the Victim Trap*

A couple of months after I ended our relationship, the telephone rang and "Northwestern Hospital" appeared on the caller ID. Somehow, I intuitively knew it was Jeff. Resolute, I refused to pick up the phone.

Tragically, months later I discovered his obituary online. Jeff died in 2007 at forty-two; his body had deteriorated from years of extreme alcohol consumption. I cried for weeks, mourning the passing of this man's illustrious soul. The disease had won while everybody else had lost. Distressingly, I also knew I had told him to "pass over" and then missed the only opportunity I'd ever have to say good-bye, because I didn't know he was standing on the precipice of death. Jeff's mother also died the following year from diabetes and medical complications.

Instead of showing me partnership and joy, this intimate union displayed my frailties. According to Benedict, learning lessons is probably the most critical part of our life path and a means to reach higher consciousness even though they can be incredibly heart-wrenching. Due to the traumatic nature of our relationship, I truly embodied the kernels of my education, absorbing each vital lesson within every cell. I felt quite sure I would not need to repeat these anytime soon.

Journal Entry

I could fill an entire chalkboard with the painful lessons I'd learned while dating Jeff, but here are the most useful ones: (1) solving another person's problems didn't make me a caring girlfriend; it made me a co-dependent, inextricably tied to a disease; (2) being completely "addicted" to love while forsaking all reason was pure madness; (3) clear boundaries are essential for a healthy relationship; (4) if something in your world does not promote well-being, use the process of "healthy detachment" and release it; and (5) hoping a person will change simply because we've asked them to will forever leave you disappointed. Real change comes only from resolving issues that lie deep within.

~ 16 ~

Finding My Guru

Suddenly, I had commercial representation and weekly on-camera auditions and consequently booked two regional television commercials. For this I was eternally grateful! It's astounding how one person can assist in fulfilling our dreams overnight.

~

Overall, my experience with Internet dating was a certifiable disaster. Having been single for several years, I'd watched the same group of middle-aged men in shiny European shoes and women in busty designer dresses cruise downtown in search of Mr. and Ms. Right. It was time for me to get off the "turnstile." So, after the devastating events with Jeff, I officially took myself out of the dating scene.

I also read a transformative book that assisted me in the healing process. *Living through the Meantime*, by Iyanla Vanzant, utilizes a house metaphor to help readers move from the "basement" of feeling betrayed and rejected after ending an intimate relationship to the "attic" of feeling the luminosity of love for ourselves, first and foremost. She encourages us to roll up our sleeves and deal with the true subject that caused the heartache.

> The "meantime" is a working time. It is the 9-5 of your life to which you bring all that you have studied, learned, been told, understand, and recognize about yourself and life. The "meantime" is a time of strengthening that knowledge so that it can work through you and for you. The "meantime" is where you land when you saw it coming, did not know what to do about it, ran around frantically for a while, and finally said, "Okay! Okay! I don't like it, but I am willing to deal with it." Willingness is the key that transforms a character-developing experience into a soul-enhancing one. At the core of your soul is the essence of love!

—Iyanla Vanzant, *Living Through the Meantime*

Rob's life had settled down. He finally had found a new job and started a relationship with an earthy, stable woman. I, on the other hand, stayed at home for several months reading more self-help novels, watching television, and painting with watercolors, my new bucket-list hobby. Nonetheless, in this quiet period, I found a delightful change. It was exactly what Vanzant promoted in her manuscript . . . the marvelous serenity of my own company. I treasured my space and alone time. I was upbeat, yet serene and required no one else for my entertainment. I put my focus back where it belonged, on the family, marketing, and acting.

Consequently, I was also fortunate enough to land a marketing dream project, a business branding program with a ten-minute training video. I was hired to write, produce, cast, and direct a corporate masterpiece. This was the first time I would be able to professionally marry my business skills with performing arts. The project had an aggressive time line and required late hours, but I never complained, not even once. Through the casting process, I worked directly with Chicago talent agencies and union actors. It fueled my fire and inspired me to stake a claim in the acting community.

Over the past years, I'd been cast in five community theater performances and although tremendously happy about the opportunities, I was tired of footing the bill. Community theater actors were required to pay one hundred fifty dollars to join the cast and also paint sets, print programs, sell tickets, and clean the bathrooms before each production. It was time for me to stop walking around on the perimeter of the acting playground.

I set a new manifestation intention. "I want to become part of the commercial scene in Chicago and get paid to act in commercials, theater, and eventually film. To be more specific, if I can make even as much as twenty-five dollars for my time, I'll consider myself a professional actor."

Chicago is home to more than two thousand experienced actors and I was on the bottom of the heap. I didn't have anything: monologue, head shot, résumé, or an agent. Undaunted, I paid a photographer to take a few head shots, prepared an acting résumé featuring my recent musical theater roles, and mailed packages out to over twenty Chicago agents.

One by one, the responses filed in: "No." "No, thank you." "We regret to inform you . . ." "Try again next year."

I was ceremoniously rejected by most of the agents in town; others never bothered to reply. After resubmitting for six months, I figured it was time to give up. *I'm never going to make it into this competitive acting circle.*

But then one day, I received a call from an agent who invited me to audition in her office on the south side of Chicago. I showed up on time and let out a little yelp as the woman pushed the video-record button. I sprang to my feet and started ranting and raving like Betty the Loon in *The Effect of Gamma Rays on Man-in-the-Moon Marigolds*. I leaned forward to bow and noticed that she was biting her lip and tracing a circle on the clipboard. Figuring I'd botched the only opportunity I would ever get, I gathered my purse and slunk toward the door.

The agent piped up, "You're still green, but if you're willing to pay for a listing on our website, we'll represent you."

At first I thought to myself, *Wow, that's pretty slimy. I have to pay cash to get listed with a talent agent?* But then I saw through the fuzzy haze. This was a monumental Brass Ring Moment. "Sure, sounds fine to me!" I declared. I wrote out a check for one hundred dollars and was listed on the agent's website within a week.

Sometimes, being opportunistic pays off. Four weeks later, the flaky agent booked me on a Comcast commercial as "background." I showed up beaming, ready to do anything for television land. But instead of performing, I spent the full day in a small holding area with forty other bored extras. We sat on folding chairs in a tightly cramped lounge with a box of granola bars, Dixie cups, and a sink. At the end of seven long hours, the director called us all onto the set for our big moment.

In the first scene, the actors were placed side-by-side on a large carved-oak staircase. The director instructed, "Pretend you are listening to a small Indian man, a spiritual guru!" I cupped my hand over my right ear and leaned forward. "Quiet on set! Action! Cut!" This took five minutes.

For scene two, we were instructed to carry the petite Indian fellow around like a rock star who'd jumped off a concert stage. I held the man's arm high in the air as we marched his stiff body in a circle. The director grabbed his bullhorn again, "Thank you, everyone. That's a wrap." I thought to myself, *That was a really stupid way to spend the day. Is this the acting career I wanted so badly?* Regardless, I received a check for eighty-nine dollars and exceeded my goal. So now I was a professional actor.

Before leaving, I made a trip to the ladies' room. This ended up being the most fortuitous event of my day. In the bathroom, I met a woman who looked like a porcelain angel, the kind who sits on top of a Christmas tree. She had straight fine blond hair, creamy skin, crystal blue eyes, and long thin legs. I wanted to hate her, but I couldn't. She spoke in an amiable lilt, "Hi, my name is Patti."

Patti was everything I wanted to be: a frequently booked Chicago actor with multiple agents and an impressive commercial career. She was also the mother of a three-year-old boy and lived in a nearby suburb. While washing hands, Patti serendipitously offered to help me break into the Chicago market and teach me a critical on-camera skill, the ear prompter.

This stupendous offer was an opportunity of a lifetime and I jumped on it. In exchange, I promised to help Patti develop marketing materials for her growing business. We swapped numbers on a paper towel right as the production crew came in to shoo us out.

From that day on, Patti became my guru. She taught me technical acting skills and marched me around the streets of Chicago, introducing me to her five agents. Like magic, they all signed me up free of charge, as it should be. Suddenly, I had commercial representation and weekly on-camera auditions and consequently booked two regional television commercials. For this I would be eternally grateful! It's astounding how one person can assist in fulfilling our dreams overnight.

Similarly, I got a call from a community-theater acting friend, Ann. She told me about a Chicago playhouse that was seeking an actress for a challenging role, a heroine who would experience a complete metamorphosis. The character had to move from being a frumpy, depressed, heartbroken gal to a foxy middle-aged dynamo with a steamy, provocative monologue. *Wow, this part was written for me!* I called the Prop Theatre and scheduled an audition with Stefan, one of the city's most brilliant and talented directors. Shortly thereafter, he booked me in my first paying theater gig.

Never before had such magical experiences dropped into my lap. The manifestation process was definitely working, but in a new way. New team members were actively appearing and assembling remarkable opportunities. Both Patti and Ann were guides, offering assistance in the flight forward. They were there to share a special gift and all I had to do was grab the handle and run with it.

Mr. Goodbar

I didn't mind breaking up with him, but what's our world coming to when a forty-five-year-old man breaks up with a forty-four-year-old woman in a text? The nerve!

~

In the "meantime," my days were calm, but my nights were strangely plagued by a recurring nightmare. Around two o'clock in the morning, a large image of Jeff's head would appear in my dream. He flew toward me at full speed, veiled in a hazy charcoal cloud, and tried to push himself inside my mouth. I punched and kicked wildly. "No, I won't let you!" I thrashed and woke up, hitting and kicking the bedcovers off. This happened three nights in a row and left me quaking in terror.

I scheduled a second visit to Mel to interpret the frightful nightmares. Mel began our session with yet another disturbing announcement. "Jeff may be dead, but he refuses to go into the Light. He's still very much attached to you. Do I have your permission to help get rid of him on your behalf?"

Willingly, I agreed. Mel closed his eyes, waved a quartz crystal spire, and started to chant a bizarre Hawaiian spell. He abruptly puffed cigarette smoke in my face and then sat back, announcing, "He's gone." I'm not really sure the spell did anything, but somehow I felt better. (And consequently, the nightmares stopped.)

Then, my unconventional psychic wanted to discuss a more pressing topic, my dating track record or lack thereof. Stubbornly I announced, "I hate men and I'm done for good. Life is much more enjoyable without them. I just want you to tell me about the important things, like marketing and acting."

Mel chortled. "Sorry, Blanche, Spirit has other plans for you." He grabbed his fountain pen and started drawing an image. "You'll meet a tall man at a business social event. He's from somewhere in Europe, with hazel eyes and dark-colored hair. He is a business guy, in finance or marketing, extremely intelligent and generous with his money. He likes a nice glass of wine but is *not* an alcoholic. The two of you are opinionated and will fight and even break up for a while, but the love will make up for it." A smile broke across his face and he clapped his hands like a child. "I see a wedding cake."

Mel handed me a line drawing of a man's head. I stared at it, repeating, "I hate men. Why are you giving this to me?"

Mel snapped, "Honey, you're not done. You're going to meet two other guys before this one comes along. So, stop complaining and get going!"

I continued to argue like a spoiled brat, "I don't want to meet someone from Europe. And tell me, why do we fight?"

Mel closed his eyes and feverishly waved his hands back and forth as if I'd irritated the gods. I sat quietly for the remainder of the session, staring at the picture in front of me.

If I had to go back on the market, this time, it was going to be on *my terms*. I knew enough about the manifesting process to do it correctly. So just like the house-hunting process, I compiled a comprehensive list of the mental, spiritual, emotional, and physical qualities I would require for a long-term partnership.

Journal Entry

I want to meet someone who is genuine, caring, strong-minded, intelligent, positive, upbeat, educated, and financially successful. He will actively pursue me, support my choices, be faithful, committed, and metaphysically open. I want him to be spontaneous, playful, adventuresome, travel-seeking, and to enjoy water sports. I want my partner to be in healthy physical shape, over five foot ten, forty-five years old or younger, with a nice head of hair. Together we are very affectionate. He is good with the children and willing to go dancing. It would be nice if he owned a car, an apartment downtown, and didn't have a crazy ex-wife, but those features are flexible.

I also created a virtual tool for screening candidates. I called it the "Date Over Meter." If a guy wasn't the whole enchilada, I'd dump him like a hot tamale. If a future prospect didn't meet even one of my requirements, I would immediately heed the imaginary neon pink Date Over sign flashing across my forehead and politely turn him down. No harm done.

If desperation is a man-repellent, disdain is a man-magnet. Without even trying, I met Ken, a tall blond accountant. His personality was stiff, but he was smart, pleasant, and had huge biceps from playing competitive tennis. He was the father of two young boys and resided in the center of Chicago's "Viagra Triangle," the night-life district where mature men and women visit watering holes in search of dates. Ken had a seemingly fanatical ex-wife, but I liked him.

We dated for several weeks and took things slow, I mean really slow. Ken was so consumed with work, ten-nis, and his boys, he barely had time for me. To make matters worse, he rarely called during the week to keep our connection alive.

After four weeks of neglect, I scheduled a dinner to give my dating companion some feedback. "Ken, you are a fantastic guy, but I'd give you a two out of ten on a personal-communication scale. I feel like I am a low pri-ority to you and I can't continue to go out with someone who doesn't keep in touch."

Ken glanced up at me, uncomfortably stirring his pad Thai noodles. He sheepishly said, "Dianne, I talk to you more than any other woman I've met in the past five years." He blinked several times. "I think you're really great and I promise to call more." I believed both state-ments and we went on to have a pleasant evening.

Two days later, I received this text: "I'M HEADING OUT FOR A TENNIS TOURNAMENT. THIS JUST ISN'T GOING TO WORK. WE SHOULD TAKE A BREAK. KEN." I didn't mind breaking up with him, but what's our world coming to when a forty-five-year-old man breaks up with a forty-four-year-old woman in a text? The nerve! The audacity!

Who does he think he is? I roiled with middle-aged self-righteous indignation.

Still, I chose not to respond because I knew there was no point. Ken was just a "glimpse," a close facsimile of my future partner; he was definitely not the whole enchilada. I made a mental note to add "healthy communication frequency" onto my growing list of partner attributes and carried on.

The next gentleman showed up on my radar screen a few weeks later. Sam was a lively, educated, fun-loving guy who was very proud of his extremely muscular body. He invited me to join him for a Halloween house party along with a group of wild forty-something friends. I relish wearing costumes, so I dressed up as Cinderella in a hoop skirt, long auburn wig, full cheery makeup, and sweeping pink gown. My date showed up as a pimp.

At the party, I met Sam's grown-up friends and watched as they drank excessively, and I smelled something funny when I walked down the narrow hall to the bathroom. I pulled Sam over into the corner of the kitchen and whispered with concern, "Do you smell that? Is someone smoking a joint?"

He twisted his nose into a ball and boisterously spit in my face, "What?!! Nobody can accuse my friends of doing drugs! I'm not even going to discuss this topic with you, ever!"

The Date Over sign flashed hot crimson. I don't hang out with drug users and this guy needed anger management classes, stat! I spent the rest of Halloween munching at the snack table, meeting a few nice single ladies, and dancing with Zorro, who dropped a phone number into my hand for a late-night hookup. I shrugged it all off. The weirdest part was, Sam asked me out for a second date. Of course, I politely turned him down.

Since my dating prospects were unimpressive, I'll admit, I fantasized quite a bit. What if I reconnected with the true love of my life from when I was a teenager? Would we feel the same rapture while falling into each other's arms? I'd not spoken to Jim in almost twenty-five years, but with the help of aids like Oprah and the Internet, people everywhere were doing it . . . finding old flames who'd once set their hearts ablaze.

I imagined that Jim was a tenured university professor, handsome and distinguished with a little gray at the temple. His eyes were still penetratingly blue. In my dream, he delivered philosophy lectures at Harvard and lived in a well-appointed New England Colonial. His pretty wife and five children visited him often for picnic lunches on the "yard."

These days, everyone's on the grid through Facebook, LinkedIn, or at least a high school registry. So I started searching for Jim, ready to pick up the phone and actually make the call. Surprisingly, I could find only two things: a newspaper article discussing his teaching endeavors in Guam and a single-sentence obituary. I discovered that Jim had been a high school teacher in the South Pacific and died four years earlier, at the age of forty-three. The news hit me like a ton of bricks. I was crushed! We were supposed to find each other and relive our transcendent passion.

I became obsessed with learning more about Jim and the life I'd missed out on. I researched the school in Guam, called to get the principal's email address, and sent this man, a total stranger, a heartfelt letter requesting information. Miraculously, I stumbled upon the ideal contact, because Craig had been Jim's friend for over twenty years.

Just as I had suspected, Jim had been a brilliant English literature teacher, a visionary in the educational field. But shockingly, his friend also categorized him as an adventure-seeking playboy with four wives, no children, and a vagabond style, moving frequently between Saipan, Guam, and China. Jim was in Tianjin, China, teaching and living in the teachers' barracks at Harbor View School when one day, he didn't show up for class. They found him dead in bed, allegedly from a heart attack. His death is still steeped in mystery. Jim's mother received a "surprise" box in the mail with his ashes and she continues to grieve to this day.

According to Craig, "Truly, the fact that he's gone is too bad, because he was a gem of a guy and no one was ever going to match his talents in the classroom. Most people wanted to kick his ass. It was just the beer and the women that kept screwing him up."

Upon receiving the letter, I went numb. For my entire adult life, I'd kept the projected hope of loving this man sewn into the base of my soul. Talk about making assumptions! My romantic imaginary tale was a trick that I'd been playing on myself; it had nothing to do with Jim or his path. Oddly, I also noted the sobering fact that both Jim and Jeff had strikingly similar and unhappy lives. Perhaps dating Jim as an adult would have been just like dating Jeff, but now I'll never know.

Several weeks after learning about Jim's fate, I met up with three Northwestern alumni girlfriends at the Chicago Sheraton Hotel for a Kellogg graduate mixer, ready for some heady intellectual dialogue and networking. By the time I'd arrived, my friends had already encircled the only attractive single man at the event. Since now I clearly had no interest in chasing men, I stubbornly refused to join their flirt circle and got busy meeting business executives and mingling with potential clients.

Eventually, the mixer came to a close and I swept over to the center of the room to collect my friends. "We're moving on to P.J. Clarke's for a late-night adventure and some fun."

There, seated on a barstool among my friends was a young Dutch financial consultant. He was wearing a navy suit, crisp French blue dress shirt, and a tan beaded necklace. I couldn't help myself. I reached out and grabbed the unusual jewelry around his neck. I commented with total sass, "You can't possibly be a Big Eight consultant and wear Rastafarian beads."

He laughed, stood up, and moved closer. I noticed his shiny coffee-colored hair, chiseled chin, and wire-frame glasses. I wasn't interested.

"Let's go, ladies. Our next destination awaits."

I poured my friends into a cab as they chimed in unison, "You just ditched the Dutch guy." I could have cared less.

We all quickly settled into P.J.'s, one of Chicago's old, dark tin-ceiling bars, and raised our glasses to nothing in particular. A few minutes later, much to my surprise, a tall man made a beeline for me. It was the Dutch guy. *Didn't I just leave him at the hotel? Did he follow us?* Enthusiastically, he pried about my business and family life, wanting to know about my kids. We talked for a few minutes and then I felt a gentle tap on my right shoulder. I spun around and stood face-to-face with Ken's best friend, Dan.

Dan greeted me gregariously and innocently asked, "So what's up with Ken these days? Will he be joining you soon?"

My eyes flooded open wide. I sputtered, "Is this a joke?" He repeated the question.

The nerve endings in my body wrenched as a long-repressed lightning bolt rushed between my teeth. I screeched, "Ken broke up with me via text message. Do you want to see it?" I waved my cell phone in his face, ranting and raving about the crime with the pale glow of the saved message beaming across the bar. My spontaneous outburst surprised even me.

Dan stood like a statue, not knowing how to handle the woman his best friend had electronically dumped. He choked in fear, "I think Ken is on his way over here right now!"

I huffed, "Bring it on!"

Dan looked behind me and swallowed hard. "He just saw your back and ran out the door."

I threw my head back and squealed like an angry boar, pushing my way through the crowd to the entrance. Ken was gone. "What a wimp!" I bellowed out the door.

Based on my strong emotional flare-up, obviously, I had not yet processed the breakup properly. I returned to Dan and apologized profusely for acting like such a shrew. The man kindly offered, "I'm leaving now. Can I offer you a ride somewhere?"

I boldly announced, "No, thanks. I have a new boyfriend and we were just heading out." I spun around and grabbed the arm of the Dutch gentleman who'd been watching our entire encounter. Dutch handed me my coat and in classic Hollywood style we sauntered out, arm-in-arm. Albeit fake, I hoped Dan would deliver the message that I'd swiftly and successfully found another man.

Several paces down the street, my new European escort cautiously inquired, "Was that a potential suitor?"

"No, it was just a poor guy who was in the wrong place at the wrong time. Thanks for helping me with the ruse. What's your name again?"

He replied, "My name is Aldert."

I took Aldert to a quiet coffee shop and explained everything; he smiled and laughed wholeheartedly. We spent some time together sipping tea and discovered something unexpected: our parallel lives. Aldert was eight years younger but we both had resided in the same suburb during high school, had lived in the same dorm at Marquette University, had attended Northwestern for graduate school and had chosen the field of consulting, and our fathers were both successful corporate CEOs in the financial field. The synergy was overwhelming.

Aldert was bright and geeky, which made him appear both mature and immature at the same time. He explained that due to his extensive work-related travel, he'd maintained only short-term relationships with women in the past and asked me to share with him some wisdom regarding how to get a girl and keep her interested. I gladly complied.

I started with the obvious: "It's good idea to read *Men Are from Mars, Women Are from Venus* because our species are very different." Then I spouted a host of useful tidbits from the book.

> One of the biggest differences between men and women is how they cope with stress. Men become increasingly focused and withdrawn while women become increasingly overwhelmed and emotionally involved. At these

times, a man's needs for feeling good are different from a woman's. He feels better by solving problems while she feels better by talking about the problems. Not understanding and accepting these differences creates unnecessary friction in our relationships.

—John Gray, *Men Are from Mars,
Women Are from Venus*

Aldert genuinely seemed to appreciate my input regarding the subject matter, so I expounded further, recapping Gray's central points. "In summary, men are goal-oriented and want to be 'needed' and women want to express themselves and be 'cherished.'" Eventually, the hour grew late and when I reached out to shake the tall businessman's hand, he leaned forward and quickly kissed me on the lips.

He recited rule number one: "A man needs to show interest right away if he likes a girl. I am definitely interested." This guy had been wearing his research hat and downloaded the "How to Date Dianne Manual."

As prescribed, Aldert sent me a genial text later that night, called me periodically throughout the week, and asked me out for a weekend date. It was refreshing to meet a refined gentleman who, unlike Ken, could actually use the telephone.

We met at a sassy Moroccan restaurant for our first date. The conversation flowed easily as we shared bowls of food without silverware. I asked question after question, searching for a reason to flash the Date Over sign. This man was young and without a single gray hair, so technically that made me a "cougar." Other than that, he was brilliant, caring, attentive, and open to adventure; basically, he was a diamond in the rough.

Even though Aldert met every item on my checklist, he wore oversized round silver wire-rim glasses and bore a strong resemblance to an adult version of Harry Potter. I think most women would agree: Harry Potter is not romantically attractive. But before I flashed the "Not Cute" sign, I had to be sure. I took a ballsy step, "Will you take your glasses off so I can see what you look like without them?" Aldert squinted and shyly peeled back the frames.

I gasped. There it was: the image from Mel's drawing. He had the same rectangular jaw, the brushed dark hair, the sharp nose, and the large green eyes, all of which had been masked by the dorky spectacles. Superman was sitting behind a Clark Kent exterior.

Mel's prediction had been entirely accurate. We started dating shortly thereafter and I found all the partnership qualities that I'd fully detailed on my list. It wasn't the take-your-breath-away puppy love I'd experienced with Tom. It wasn't the frantic, crazy-infused passion I'd experienced with Jeff. It was a sound, sane, and serene union. Every weekend we'd snuggle close at jazz clubs, concerts, comedy clubs, theater events, and even *Tony n' Tina's Wedding*.

Aldert's parents lived in Amsterdam but traveled annually to California for a month-long winter vacation. We'd been seeing each other for only a few months when he invited me to join him in visiting the affluent transcontinental snowbirds.

I wanted to escape the deep January chill, but I was nervous about engaging with the noble European pair. My shunning experience with Tom's folks had left me jumpy. So, I created a brief affirmation to remind me of my unique, lovable qualities: "I am gracious, friendly, fun, clever, and outgoing. What's there not to like?" *And, there's no way I could have such formidable foes again, right?*

Aldert's aristocratic mother and patrician father greeted us at the Oceanside condo with stiff double-cheek kisses. They were dressed in posh upscale attire and spoke impeccable English. In a very progressive style, they showed us to our bedroom, an open second-floor loft with a king-size bed overlooking the family room. This was going to be interesting.

After unpacking, we all took a seat in the well-appointed living room. It was as if Queen Elizabeth and Prince Philip had invited me to Buckingham Palace for tea. After only a few minutes of introductory dialogue, Aldert's mother sat up stiffly and in proper royal style commented, "Divorces are always so painful. It produces nothing but sadness. I know families that have never recovered." I was immediately on the hot seat.

As a professional communicator, I am pretty talented at dodging bullets; I hastily changed the subject. I yanked a picture from my hip pocket, hoping to win over the matriarch with the chaste faces of my children, and offered, "They all have straight A's. I am very proud of them." The mention of my kids made the Dutch momma bear freeze; the hairs on her arms visibly bristled. She was not ready to face the single-mom reality check. I grabbed back the picture and rammed it into my pocket, changing the subject once again.

"Let's go explore San Diego together over the next few days. What do you like to do?"

Aldert's parents shook their heads in unison. His dad flatly replied, "We spend our days playing cards poolside and occasionally take in a round of golf." This wasn't going well. I don't play golf and prefer vigorous sports like body surfing and hiking, or visiting amusement parks. I also pride myself in discovering local hot spots. Unfortunately, I didn't have a car, so I was stuck. Aldert's mother then turned away and delivered a long commentary in Dutch. I understand both French and German, so I was fairly certain she was talking about me, and it didn't sound flattering. Regardless, I played completely dumb.

For the next two days, Aldert reclined poolside next to his parents, speaking Dutch and working with a computer on his lap. I swam back and forth in the pool, took long solitary walks on the beach, picked up shells, meditated, and watched the surfers. I felt great sympathy for Princess Diana. She must have experienced harsh parental judgment from hoity Queen Lizzy.

I kept my tongue quiet for three days, and on the fourth begged Aldert to take me away to Catalina for an overnight. I knew the side trip would increase my lack of popularity, but I desperately needed to remember why we were dating in the first place. He agreed and we spent two superb days exploring the quiet Pacific island retreat whale-watching, hiking, and shopping like normal vacationing lovebirds. After returning to the condo, the shunning parental chill was stifling, but again, I acted as if I didn't notice.

Aldert had planned to stay in California for a few extra days. So, while he chauffeured me to the airport, I mustered up the courage to ask him the question I'd undoubtedly been avoiding all week: "What do your parents think of me?"

My boyfriend cleared his throat and began with a disclaimer. "Dutch people are blunt, and even though my parents hold strong opinions, it doesn't mean I feel the same." I clung to the cheap rental-car upholstery and braced myself. "My parents are worried because you're older and that I'll need to care for you as you age. My father is hurt because he wanted me to carry on the family name with my own children. They also think your personality is a bit strong."

For the second time, I'd been judged as old, barren, and headstrong. The sting from their weighty disapproval was almost overwhelming. Once again my Emotional Child was bruised. Where were my adoring future father and mother-in-law?

According to Don Miguel Ruiz's *The Four Agreements*, there are four rudimentary steps to personal freedom: (1) always do your best, (2) be impeccable with your word, (3) don't make any assumptions, and (4) don't take anything personally.

> Don't take anything personally. What others say and do is a projection of their own reality, their own dream. When you are immune to the opinions and actions of others, you won't be the victim of needless suffering.

—Don Miguel Ruiz, *The Four Agreements*

These principles are genuinely solid and highly recommended as an approach for life, though they are not always easy to practice. On our trip, I followed the first agreement and tried to do my best by remaining pleasant, open, and understanding. Everything else, however, I did completely wrong. I'd not been honest with my word. In fact, I'd kept all of my thoughts and feelings bottled up.

I'd made thousands of false assumptions about his parents, their thoughts, feelings, and actions. I also took everything personally, especially the jab about taking care of me in the nursing home as I age. I simply didn't possess the skills to allow stabbing feedback to roll off my back. *Why had this issue resurfaced? Is the Universe telling me to walk away and return the Netherland Prince back to his chateau?*

When Aldert got back to Chicago, we fought like two young children, each battling to defend our own insecurities. Aldert felt like the "bad" son, the family disappointment, because he didn't have plans to reproduce. And since I wanted to be part of his loving extended family, I couldn't deal with the disapproval from the couple I'd truly hoped would care for me as a daughter.

As Mel had predicted, Aldert and I fought hard. I questioned, "Are you a man or an infant? If you can't tell your parents to keep their opinions to themselves, perhaps you should go back home and hang off your mother's bosom!" And I stormed out, breaking up with him for a week.

But just like Romeo and Juliet, as soon as his parents flew back to Amsterdam, we ran back together and swept our issues under the rug: Aldert's need to please his parents and my inability to confront negativity directly and accept my tomato throwers without launching into an emotionally charged harangue. But as we all know, if you don't address your lessons, the issues don't go away, they just hide away until another day.

≈

SECTION VI

Authenticity

≈

⁀ 18 ⁀

Truth Will Set You Free

I grew up in an overly strict household and learned how to craft white lies, stories, and socially appropriate excuses to avoid outbursts or critiques. It was time to step forward and enter a critical phase of truth-telling. I had to come squeaky clean with my community and in all of my intimate relationships.

⌁

According to Ruiz, "Impeccability of the word can lead you to personal freedom, success, and abundance." I'd finally found my heart in a loving, secure partnership, but I was still utterly out of integrity. I knew it would be impossible for me to truly experience joy until I learned how to say everything that had to be said. I had to release the hounds of full expression and speak my truth in all areas of life. *But how do I articulate authentic feelings and desires in the moment, no matter what?*

I was a well-trained honesty sweeper. I grew up in an overly strict household and learned how to craft white lies, stories, and socially appropriate excuses to avoid outbursts or critiques. It was time to step forward and enter a critical phase of truth-telling. I had to come squeaky clean with my community and in all of my intimate relationships.

Conscious Living by Gay and Kathlyn Hendricks became my bible. This phenomenal book recommends building a solid existence by recognizing the issues that emerge, forming agreements, and practicing "microscopic truth-telling." Gay Hendricks recommends living each moment by committing to the truth within:

> The most common feelings: you are mad about something or sad or scared or joyful, and you haven't given yourself the ten seconds of pure attention to it that will allow it (and most feelings) to resolve. In other words, you haven't told yourself the full truth about it, and you haven't told the relevant other person or persons. This act of lying to yourself and others puts a wobble in your whole being that can only be smoothed out through full communication.
>
> —Gay and Kathlyn Hendricks, *Conscious Living: Finding Joy in the Real World*

Considering my enormous marriage cover-up, I had a lot of "wobbles" in my world. Now, it was essential that I learn how to scrub my tongue and say *yes* when I meant *yes* and *no* when I meant *no*. I also had to experiment with establishing healthy boundaries to avoid the chaos that had developed in past relationships.

I began by practicing with a scary group, the North Shore parochial school system. I started with the nun. I told the head of our private Catholic school, "No, Sister, I am not going to buy magazines, gift-wrap paper, raffle tickets, spaghetti dinners, or poinsettias from the annual school drives anymore. We don't need that stuff and can't afford it." She seemed to understand.

I moved on to the school moms. These women spend every waking moment "hover-crafting" over the small private educational institution, demanding full compliance for their excessive activities. Parents who do not participate are bombarded with "lack of compliance" emails to publically shame and blame the culprit. I spoke my truth anyway. "I'm sorry, but I'm not going to attend the eighth-grade orientation coffee. I've been at this school for over a decade and I don't need an orientation. And unlike everyone else, our finances are tight and I work. I simply don't have mornings for leisure." At least superficially, they seemed to accept my response.

And, when a neighbor invited my son over to join her boy for a play date, I told her the "real" reason Adam couldn't hang out. "Nicholas has a lot of positive energy, but the last time he was at our house, I overheard him using a slew of inappropriate swear words. I don't want Adam to hear that kind of talk." The request for play dates stopped.

Eventually, I moved my clear, sparkling expression to a whole new level. While I was living quietly in the suburbs practicing honesty, many of my single friends were still onboard the party train chasing the night. Sue, one of the first girlfriends I had met while newly single, invited me to join her downtown for a wild St. Patrick's

Day party. Although I loved Sue, and St. Patty's Day, for that matter, I'd spent too many nights escorting this woman home stumbling drunk. After witnessing Jeff's disease, I had no choice but to express my grave concern. "Sue, you're a fantastic person, but I can't hang out with you because you drink to excess. Your face turns sour and dark, and you start to slur. I'm also worried about your safety when you come home alone at night in that condition. Perhaps you should consider AA for some help." She cried on the phone and admitted, she too was terribly afraid for her future.

Even my friendship with Lori needed some straightening out. Every time we'd plan a get-together, she'd ask me to pick her up on my way downtown. At first, I didn't mind, because it gave us more time to talk, but after consistent trials, I discovered a pervasive issue: her lack of punctuality. No matter how often I sent her updates with my arrival time, I'd sit inside my car on a busy Chicago street with flashers blinking while she primped. My blood boiled, especially after a thirty-minute delay. This was the perfect opportunity for me to set some boundaries. I expressed myself openly. "Girlfriend, when I drive down to pick you up, you're not ready. I wait outside for you like a private limo driver and get so annoyed, it ruins my night." She got the message. We agreed to meet at events in the future, a much healthier option.

But not everyone appreciated my candor. Over the years, Carrie and I had spent many nights together out on the town. I'd worked hard to maintain my "wing girl" status even though it was hard to do. I enjoyed Carrie as a driven, educated woman but she was also exacting and demanding. One night, she invited me to P.J. Clarke's for happy hour and sliders. Since I had not seen her in months, I was delighted that we could spend some quality time together. While waiting for burgers, an attractive young man sauntered up to our table. He started a lively conversation with us and after ten minutes left to join a group of his friends on the other side of the bar.

As soon as the man walked away, Carrie squared me off, screeching in my face, "I can't believe you cock-blocked me!" Yes, I talked to the young attractive man, but I didn't really know what the term *cock-block* meant. The bottom line was, I was fed up with this woman's bossiness and I needed to openly articulate my pent-up exasperation. "I don't like it when you speak to me like that, especially about a random stranger. Your words are controlling and over the top. For a long time I've been afraid to express myself with you because I thought you'd lash out and bully me. I know a lot of your other friends also feel the same way." As soon as I finished my sentence, Carrie stood up and walked out of P.J. Clarke's, leaving me with the tab.

I knew my message was harsh, but honestly, I thought we'd eventually kiss and make up. Instead, Carrie officially dumped me. According to an old adage, "Friends are there for a reason, a season, or a lifetime." I guess she was only there for a season. I stewed, wondering if I'd made a dreadful mistake by breaking my silence. But with time, I eventually understood the hidden gift that had emerged from her exit. I learned an invaluable lesson: Micro-truthing didn't allow me to control the outcome. Some people would be able to accept moment-to-moment truth and share in mutually beneficial dialogue, and others would flee. Regardless, either way I would become more "impeccable" and clean.

Aldert was next on my list for scouring. He traveled every week from Monday at dawn until late Thursday night. I'd race downtown to his apartment every Thursday night and pace back and forth like a caged lioness until his plane landed from Washington, Atlanta, Seattle, or some other city. Sometimes it didn't land at all.

As the months progressed, I developed a vicious cycle from childhood: On Monday I was fine. On Tuesday, I started to feel empty and alone. By Wednesday, I was furious with him for being gone for so long. By Thursday, I was cold and despondent, picking fights. My Abandoned Child cried, *What about my needs? When do I get another hug? Aren't I important?*

I tried everything to make my fanatical emotions stop, but they hastily escalated, spinning into an erratic tornado. I addressed him straight on: "Aldert, it's no surprise that you haven't had any long-term relationships. I feel like I'm dating a traveling salesman. I'm not equipped to handle my own internal roller coaster and I can't stay with you if you don't eventually make plans to stop traveling. Can you please ask your boss for a consulting project in Chicago?"

Aldert admitted that he too was tired of living out of a suitcase and assured me he'd request a local client for his next project. I settled back down again as he flew off to San Francisco.

❦ 19 ❦

The Reveal

But like a cancer, lies gnaw, grow, and eventually decompose the healthy fibers of every relationship. There's never a "good" time to tell someone you have been lying to them for three years. We simply had to face what we dreaded most, confronting the children.

~

Over the past few months, Alexandra had begun asking questions about her parents' unusual behavior. "Why don't you and Dad go out together? Why do you always go out alone?" I'd artfully dodge the bullet: "Dad and I are friends and we like to do different things. What do you want for dinner?" Rob and I were both in steady, committed relationships and it was finally time to reveal our separation to the three little people we adored.

I approached Rob and articulated my intention to tell the kids everything. He violently disagreed. "For over three years we've kept our separation as the perfect secret, why tell them now?" He was spot on. We'd done an outstanding job of masquerading as a married couple. But like a cancer, lies gnaw, grow, and eventually decompose the healthy fibers of every relationship. There's never a "good" time to tell someone you have been lying to them for three years. We simply had to face what we dreaded most, confronting the children.

I planned everything. I picked the first day of spring break so the kids would be out of school and found a therapist for our sensitive, hormonal thirteen-year-old and a Hoffman-based life coach for my own moral support. I also contacted the kids' homeroom teachers asking for support as well as some of their classmates' parents. I even wrote a brief script and practiced it. I was ready.

On the day of our scheduled tell-all, I performed mindless busy work, nervously sweating until nightfall. Then right before bedtime, Rob and I asked the children to join us in the recreation room. "Have a seat. Your father and I have something to tell you." *Isn't that how bad news always starts?* I delivered the blow, "You guys probably had noticed that your father and I don't spend much time together. We're friends but don't have the special kind of relationship needed to be a husband and wife. We will always love you, but we are separated and it's been that way for quite a while. Eventually we'll get divorced, but for now we'll all stay together in this house, as long as we can afford it." I held my breath, bracing for Hiroshima.

I sat there watching Alexandra as her consciousness lifted from her body. In a flash, she jumped off the couch and started wailing, waterworks spraying across the room. She paced back and forth like a hamster on a wheel ranting about a divorce premonition. "I had a dream. I saw this coming. I knew you'd do this." She made jerky catatonic oversized body movements, howling, "You're trying to kill me. You've ruined my life."

Emma, who was nine, moved into her left brain. She fired questions, carefully trying to calculate the impact. "Why don't you just keep everything like it is? We don't care if you don't spend time together. Why do you have to get divorced? Why is Alexandra screaming?"

Four-year-old Adam started whimpering and fell to the floor rolling around and around. He didn't understand what was happening, but he felt the shock waves cascading throughout the room. Rob sat on the couch immobilized, eyes fixated on the floor. It was a horrid scene.

Alexandra's mind fast-forwarded. She shrieked, "I don't care if you guys get divorced, but we all have to live together! And you can never ever date anyone else!" She pointed an angry index finger at me. "I will murder anyone you bring into this house." She sprinted to her bedroom and slammed the door, cracking the plaster down two floors below.

I followed. Thank goodness, doors in the old Georgian didn't have locks. She roared when I barged in, "Leave! Get out of here. I hate you. You've ruined us."

I bravely took a seat at the end of her bed and calmly stated, "You can say and do anything you want, but I'm going to stay here, no matter what. I will help you through this."

She sat up and violently rocked like an autistic child holding her head and chanting, "This isn't real. I'm in a dream. I am not really here. I have to wake up." She threw her head back with a devilish cackle. "I'm dead right now. This is another world. Where am I?" She alternated cycles between tears and madness until finally collapsing in a heap of despair. Thank God, emotions eventually ebb. If the tirade hadn't eventually stopped, I surely would've had a nervous breakdown.

Emma came in and sat down on Alex's bed. She wanted more information. I explained, "Very little will change in your day-to-day life. You guys are staying at the same school and keeping all of your friends and your dad will remain in the house with us."

I took this moment to probe, "Did you notice that your father and I didn't act like married people?" The girls both nodded. "Did you wonder what was going on?" They nodded again. There was an uncomfortable moment of silence. I promised, "Everything will be okay." I didn't tell them about our "significant others" waiting in the wings. Ripping them apart with a separation and an impending divorce was good enough for one night. I simply could not inflict any more damage.

At midnight, I went back to my room and laid my head down, entirely depleted and numb. This was one of the worst experiences of my life; nothing could've prepared me for such complete devastation. I gashed my children's hearts wide open and watched while they flailed in pain. I sat like Satan on his throne, quietly observing the poor inconsolable humans fall to their knees. *How can I hurt thee? Let me count the ways.* Racked with remorse and uncertainty, I had no idea whether or not everything would be okay. The only redeeming part of this tell-all event was that I removed my mask. The truth will set you free.

For weeks, Rob and I walked around on eggshells as the kids moved through the Kubler-Ross steps of denial, anger, bargaining, and depression. To Alexandra, the strain of her parents' separation left her shattered and limp. To her, I'd become the monstrous betrayer, the hideous source of all that was evil. She wouldn't acknowledge my presence. But just like Anne Sullivan helped

Helen Keller return to the world of speech, Alexandra's skilled psychotherapist raised her back to a functioning level. After each visit, the child brightened and became more noticeably calm. Occasionally, she even smiled.

Emma, on the other hand, was quiet and shut down. She told me not to speak about the "DIV," so we didn't. She distracted herself with play dates and sporting events, showing little emotion. I think she was waiting for the next shoe to drop.

Rob's behavior also changed after the announcement. He resigned himself to the basement and became Adam's constant companion, watching endless hours of television to the exclusion of everyone else. And Adam became increasingly aggressive as a result.

I took all of it on. As the steady captain of the ocean liner of change, I shouldered Alexandra's grief, Emma's withdrawal, and Adam's anger. I laid their heartache on my body and withstood the verbal and physical outbursts. As I bore the weight of the shifting family model, my left shoulder started throbbing, waking me up every night with immense pain. I took a handful of Tylenol and told myself it would go away. Thank goodness, my sanity was refreshed by regular visits to my miraculous life coach, and I found comfort in Aldert's two strong arms on the weekends.

To make matters worse, I woke up one morning with a stabbing switchblade-like pain running across the bottom of both feet. I couldn't walk. I threw ice packs on my heels and slapped on a pair of high boots. I had to take tiny strides like a toddler, but with shortened tendons at least I could get around. This will go away, I reassured myself, and popped more over-the-counter painkillers.

Time and space helped us all settle down. The weather moved from a chilly spring to a blissful summer and the household was finally peaceful again. It was an ideal opportunity to see if my boyfriend would pass the "sniff-test." Aldert was fairly obsessive compulsive about things. After reading the mail, he would carefully put every piece of paper into a shredding machine, including the junk mail. And before leaving his apartment, he had to go through an elaborate "shut down" ritual, checking the stove and door locks multiple times. Needless to say, I had to do my research and see if this man was parenting material or not.

Therefore, I planned an outing to bring Emma and Adam downtown to meet my "friend" Aldert and swim in his apartment building's pool. When kids first arrived, Aldert acted like an awkward, stiff Dutch Autobot; he was unaccustomed to having children running around his house. But as soon as everyone hit the refreshing water, we all had great splashing fun. It went so well, I invited him to join me and the kids for a boat ride at Navy Pier along with two other little schoolmates. I was delighted to see him naturally entering into the role of protector. He carried our bags, paid for our food, cleaned up the spills, corralled the four children, and bought everyone a stuffed animal. He was a natural caregiver and I felt even more confident that my relationship would last for a fairly long time.

In August, to complete my lesson in verity I decided to deliver the final seismic bomb. With two weeks left of the summer break, I gathered the family back down in the basement and opened with, "Your father and I have something to tell you."

Alexandra started with a low rumble, "Ahhhh. Noooo!"

I calmly continued, "Both of us have other people in our lives that we care about deeply. Adam and Emma have met Aldert and your dad's friend is named Karyn. We're dating and want you to know that."

Pandemonium! This time Emma and Alexandra grabbed hands and huddled in the corner. Together they spewed venomous curses, "It's okay if Dad is seeing someone, but you're the worst mother in the world. We'll never forgive you. You promised you wouldn't go out with anyone else. We'll never listen to you again. You're wicked and horrible." They ran off back to their rooms. *Of course I didn't say I wouldn't date. How could I? It was a critical part of my mission. And, what's with the double standard?*

Again, I took the role of nasty empress, burning the cholera of lies down to the ground. Both girls flailed, flopped, and plotted Aldert's demise. They couldn't blame their mother for overhauling their world and so they blamed the new guy. Alexandra and I ran back to counseling, Emma held it all in, and Rob holed up with Adam down in the basement.

In the clear hue of hindsight, I hated myself for having been such a fearful coward. I not only made the catastrophic mistake of waiting too long to tell the kids, but I also, in their minds, revealed one nugget of information to them at a time. This just made me an untrustworthy liar. In retrospect, I should have stood up at the dinner table the moment our marriage was over and objectively declared, "Your dad and I are buddies. We're separated, dating other people, and searching for new life partners. This house is more than we can afford, but we're trying to stay here so you guys don't fall apart." It would have been a factual account.

The She-Devil started dancing on her throne with a severe reprimand: *You're supposed to be a good mother, but you're a total stupid, worthless fraud instead.* This time, I would have to agree with every word. Yet, through this devastating process, I truly learned the "impeccable" value of my word. Attempting to shield myself from the kids' painful responses caused more damage than I could've ever imagined. I would never again lie to avoid the reactions of another human being. It was absolutely not worth it.

I wanted my kids to be happy again, so I ran around making deals to soothe their hurt. Bribes have been used for centuries. Fine jewelry, dogs, cars, money, whatever it takes to get everyone to stop acting as if the world has come to an end. "What will make you feel better, Emma?"

She quickly responded with, "A puppy of my very own."

"Done!" I answered back. "What will make you feel better, Alexandra?"

"I want a car as soon as I turn sixteen," she announced.

"So be it!" I agreed. "Adam, what do to want?"

With his eyes fixated on The Wiggles as they danced across the television set, he muttered, "I want a revolver." Okay, that was the easiest request of all, just as long as it was made of plastic and not metal.

Shortly after dousing the family with the holy water of truth, Aldert was assigned to an Illinois-based client and started visiting us regularly at the house. Whenever he stepped inside, Alexandra threw her head back and moaned. She cast a frigid spell across the domicile, melodramatically stomping up the stairs. Emma was quiet and Adam merrily greeted his new friend.

Adam liked Aldert and frequently pulled him into to the basement for light saber battles. Oddly over time, the four-year-old turned every game into a wrestling match. Adam violently hit, kicked, and pounded Aldert on the chest and then moved toward me to continue the fight. Aware of his developing aggression, I signed him up for Tae Kwon Do. It was the perfect outlet for our young boy's pent-up frustration in response to our irregular household.

Plus, Mother Nature lent us a hand in uniting our evolving family unit. In October, an enormous cyclone skipped through our village. Fortunately, we were all safe, the kids and I tucked inside the house and Rob on vacation with his girlfriend. But in a matter of minutes, the torrential storm knocked down giant oaks, flooded streets, split telephone poles, and crashed tree limbs through hundreds of homes. We too were left without power. Inches of water flooded the basement and enormous branches lay across the driveway, yard, and roof.

I became Ma Ingalls on the prairie, running around gathering candles and extra blankets to withstand the nighttime chill. I quickly called Aldert on my dying cell phone. Like a knight in shining armor he commanded, "Sit tight! I'm on my way." He drove from downtown through the swollen city streets and limb-blocked passages and splashed a mile on foot to our dark house.

Crisis forced us to bond as we bunkered down in the powerless house for the next four days. The five of us had to join forces in a common cause, including chopping down branches, clearing debris, moving furniture, and emptying the now-hot fridge. Somehow, the dynamics had changed that weekend; adversity does that. Aldert moved from the family enemy to a helper.

To keep his emerging acceptance alive, Aldert also crafted a tempting offer to befriend the still-icy Alexandra. He offered her an all-expenses-paid fifteenth-birthday trip to New York City. She was reluctant, but knew it was a chance of a lifetime.

In November, Aldert flew Alexandra, Emma, and me to New York and put us up in a Times Square two-bedroom suite. He took us to *Phantom of the Opera* and *Wicked* on Broadway and out for an elaborate birthday meal. We all enjoyed the Big Apple, and Alex's new neutral attitude was a huge improvement. The trip cracked the code. It's hard to hate someone who is patient and caring, not to mention generous.

≈ 20 ≈

Deconstruction Central

It was imperative that we face all critical endings dead-on before the recession hit, including selling the property, paying off debt, settling up with my dad, and finding a new place to live.

≈

If 2007, the year of "truth-telling," was difficult, it paled in comparison to what I would face in 2008, the year of "endings." Just by its nature, the family house concept was an unsustainable falsehood. With the marriage missing from the nucleus of the home, the arrangement was merely a temporary means to avoid selling real estate and shuttling kids back and forth. I had to bring everything to closure.

Journal Entry

I keep having the same nightmare: The bell rings and I slowly open the cherry red door. A repulsive man with a wart-covered face and wrinkled suit extends his hand. I lay my keys in his leathery palm and he snatches them away. With a grimacing smirk, he walks inside our house and I skirt past with the kids in tow. The man closes the door and we all head for a homeless shelter, walking down an empty street with only the clothes on our back. I ask the three little ones to lie down on the facility's filthy, lice-ridden cots and cover them up with newspapers. There are no blankets.

I didn't need anyone to help me interpret the dream. Our household was teetering on the edge of a colossal sinkhole. Our line of credit was maxed out along with the credit cards, and we still owed my father for bailing us out. Frighteningly, national economic signs were also pointing toward decline. It was imperative that we face all critical endings dead-on before the recession hit, including selling the property, paying off debt, settling up with my dad, and finding a new place to live.

I sat Rob down and shared my plan. He was livid, screaming, "You promised that we would stay under the same roof. You told the children we would make this situation work!" He called me a litany of nasty names and slammed his fist on the counter. I scratched my head in disbelief.

I responded, flabbergasted, "Every cent we have is in this house. If housing prices drop, we'll lose the equity and we need that money to start over. Don't you understand?"

Rob stormed off, broadcasting, "I will not lift a finger to help you with this nonsense." And he didn't. That was the day our cooperative co-parenting interactions ended. Despite my metaphysical training, positive mindset, and communication techniques, we were no longer working comrades. Perhaps the rupture of this "friendship" is what was required to shut the door on a difficult sixteen-year relationship.

Authorities say that tight finances, getting divorced, job stress, and difficult personal relationships are among the top five emotional stressors. I faced them all head-on, just as Aldert revealed that he'd been reassigned to a project in California. *What happened to working in Chicago?* Apparently, I was going to have to wrap up my overly extended existence all by myself.

In the spirit of micro-truthing, I took the kids out for burgers and calmly explained, "Your dad and I are getting divorced. We have to sell the house because we can't afford to stay here. We'll find a rental home somewhere near school and your father will find a place nearby, just like other families do in this situation." This time, the kids didn't protest; they'd been waiting for the other shoe to drop, and inevitably, it did. As a consolation prize, I offered to let them decorate their new rooms. They quietly pushed their plates off to the side because they were no longer hungry.

It was May 2008 and I had to artfully sell the mini-mansion to avoid crashing prices in a puffed-up neighborhood. The only problem was, after five years of busy family life and limited cash for upkeep, the house was a ratty mess: peeling exterior paint, ripped wallpaper, handprints, scuffed wood floors, missing shutters, broken bathroom tiles, and a giant falling-down fence. There was no way I could bring the home back to a million-dollar state by myself.

I turned once again back to my manifestation skills. I decided to reach out to the grid and concentrate on team members, those individuals who'd always been supportive and encouraging. I tossed my head back and pleaded with the Universe, "Show me how to connect with others and get this work done, affordably."

Lori called me a few days later and I found myself hysterical on the line. "The house is a pit and I can't fix it all alone. I don't have much money and don't know where to turn. Do you have any ideas?" I knew she owned a busy contracting firm, but I never expected her response: "Calm down." She chirped, "This is your lucky day. I'll be traveling next month, so you can use my contracting crew at cost for your renovation. You'll be doing me a favor by keeping the guys busy while I am gone. It works out for everyone." I exhaled a noisy burst in relief.

The Universe had delivered to me the ideal team. Juan and his crew worked for a full month, painting every square inch of the dwelling, and together, we restored the residence to mint condition. I hugged each one of my new helpers, fawning, "You guys are the most wonderful people in the world." I wasn't joking. Their support was nothing short of miraculous.

Beth was no longer in the real estate business, and I needed to find a new dynamo to help me sell the house. Serendipitously during a business meeting, I mentioned to my dear friend and colleague Mike, "I just finished upgrading our home and need to list it on the market right away."

He gushed, "You have to meet Lynn, one of the top realtors on the North Shore. She's sold two of my properties and her personality is a unique combination of both sweet and assertive. She's also into New Age stuff, just like you."

I immediately followed up on his lead. I called Lynn and invited her to tour my now-magnificent homestead. Her big blue eyes twinkled as she walked through the crisp, creamy entranceway. I could tell she was excited. I sat her down at our mahogany dining-room table and explained, "I'm probably not like your typical client. I'm skilled in the Law of Abundance. I use both my mental and physical prowess to get what I want." I watched and waited to see if she flinched.

Lynn planted a smile on her freckled face and settled back into the carved oak chair. I continued, "I want an offer by August for a specific amount which I'll split equally with my to-be-ex-husband." I pushed a small piece of paper toward her with a number written on it.

Most realtors would think I was a lunatic, but Lynn responded with five magic words: "Have you ever met Mel?" This was my brass ring sign from above.

Lynn and I immediately became the dynamic duo, partners in the race to sell the property before the economy dipped. She had the house photographed and listed within a week and the floodgates opened with ten immediate showings. Rob kept his room clean and planted a few flowers in the front of the yard, but that was about it.

Whenever I announced, "Show Time!" the kids and I ran around like Tasmanian devils, straightening beds, cleaning bathrooms, wiping counters, and throwing debris into the closet. Then we'd bolt out the front door, dragging our overly protective dog behind.

I did my best to keep a lid on the stress, but it was hard to maintain a perfectly clean house with three messy kids scampering around inside. I found myself bellowing, "Who left that dirty towel on the floor? You're grounded! Fix your bedcovers! You're grounded! There's a muddy shoe print on the floor. You're all grounded for a week!"

Addressing the ongoing series of endings, I turned my attention toward legal matters. Despite our war-like stance, Rob and I had very little money for lawyers and thus agreed upon on a do-it-yourself-style divorce. Through another referral, I received the name of a highly progressive attorney who was willing to guide us through the divorce process and act as a mediator for an estimated four thousand dollars. Technically however, he could represent only one of us, which was me. For our first joint divorce meeting, I laid a spreadsheet out on the attorney's desk, featuring all our prenegotiated terms, and the man openly remarked, "Wow. I'm not going to make much money off you two."

Unashamedly, I exclaimed, "Good. I hope you don't!"

For the next four weeks, I acted like a secretary. The lawyer sent me boilerplate documents and I negotiated at home with Rob, adding new language to our developing agreement. I typed up the responses for all parties to review, emailing versions back and forth. Just when the final draft was ready for signatures, Rob decided to hire a separate lawyer. Although there was nothing ultimately wrong with this decision, it threw our ultra-cheap divorce out the window. After hundreds of lawyer-to-lawyer phone calls and two miniscule changes to the decree, our bill soared to nearly eight thousand dollars and pushed the divorce back to November. Nevertheless, the paperwork was filed.

Meanwhile, during the second week of August, we'd received three miraculous offers on the house. I felt like Goldilocks: the first offer was too soft and full of contingencies; the second, too hard with a low-ball; and the third one was just right, the exact amount requested after all fees paid and an October closing date. Lynne and I had created the flawless sale, but I didn't take time off to celebrate because I was too busy trying to find a new place to live.

As a newly single mom, I wanted to find the cheapest rental in town. So, I scouted around the suburbs and stumbled upon a bright yellow bungalow near the school with an expansive yard, full deck, and a towering oak tree for climbing. It only had three bedrooms, but the second floor sported a double-wide walk-in closet, so I got creative. If we take everything off the walls, this room is big enough to fit a six-year-old boy's twin bed and a skinny shelf. I hated to make Adam sleep in a closet, but at least everyone could have their own space. Sold!

I returned to my perpetual state of pure "doing-ness." I fixed every item on the home inspector's list and gave Rob a set of blue stickers to mark the furniture he wanted to keep. I grabbed a box of pink stickers and walked through our house as if I were at a church bazaar, scouring for antiques.

The act of shopping through my own home felt completely surreal. Every item and knickknack had a story. Nostalgically, I recalled the first significant acquisition of our marriage, the barley twist table and the Belgian armoire that we stumbled upon at Rebecca Ann's, a stuffy antique shop in Lake County. A twinge of sorrow welled up inside. I stared at the blue velvet couch we found in Muncie, Indiana, after our honeymoon. An immense tightness grabbed my throat. *Is that a tear?* I tersely booted my emotional self in the rear. *Stay focused. Keep your head up. Hey, no crying allowed!* I stuck a fingernail deep into my palm to make the gloom slither back down where it belonged.

Every day, I worked to dismantle our large dwelling, but the Universe added an unexpected event. Two weeks before moving day, I woke to the sounds of Adam coughing a full-chest rumble. He'd been fighting a cold but clearly it'd progressed. I peeked into his dimly lit room and looked upon an ashen face. He rasped from under the blankets, "Help me, Mom!" It was 7:30 a.m. on a Saturday morning and I called the pediatrician, gave Rob instructions to handle the household, and ran out in a heavy rainstorm carrying the little boy in green dinosaur pajamas. I hauled Adam across town as he heaved from the backseat, "I can't breathe. Help me!"

The nurse looked apprehensively at my sick youngster and immediately ushered us into a room to measure his oxygen level with a tight finger clamp. The doctor came in and nervously declared, "Adam has a dangerous case of asthma. He's in the red level." I gasped out loud; obviously, that was bad. For the next two hours, Adam sat on my lap watching *Bambi*, alternating between a nebulizer and oxygen tank while I studied a reference book about asthmatic children.

When the film ended, the doctor charged back in and announced, "You need to leave now and go to Glenbrook Hospital. We are in the middle of an awful storm and this area is flooded. We've made arrangements for your admission into the emergency room. Our office is now closed."

I glanced back in shock as the nurse locked the office door behind me. Somehow, during *Bambi*, a monsoon had left a lake of water as high as the running board on the SUV I'd just purchased to replace my recently broken-down sports car. I took off my shoes, rolled up my pants, and carried Adam out in the torrential storm, slopping through two feet of water and mud. By the time I clicked the child safety belt, we were both soaked.

I prayed the RAV4 would act like a proper crossover. The car sputtered, but we pulled away from the curb with a full wake, passing stalled low-riding vehicles on the side of the street.

The hospital emergency room staff hooked Adam up to a new set of machines and immediately took chest X-rays, which revealed pneumonia in both lungs. He had to be transferred to a third medical facility, the pediatric ward of Evanston Hospital by ambulance. Adam cheered. I moaned.

Adam smiled from behind the plastic mask as the sirens blared and we traveled across town. I was beyond exhausted. I called Rob and asked him to meet me at 8:00 p.m. in Adam's hospital room to cover the overnight shift so I could get some rest before returning early the next morning. This is what he said: "I have to go to a corporate holiday party with my girlfriend tonight. We've had this planned for months. It's downtown so I don't know what time I'll be back."

I screamed back, livid. "Your son needs an oxygen mask to breathe. Go to the party for an hour and I repeat, meet me at Evanston Hospital by eight!"

At dinnertime, Aldert brought Emma and Alexandra to our private room for a short visit and dropped off Adam's teddy bear, Hungry, clean pajamas, and a toothbrush. Rob sauntered into the hospital after 10:00 p.m. By that point, I was so furious my head almost exploded. I marched him into the hallway and hollered words that should never be spoken out loud to another human being. I'm surprised the hospital security staff didn't escort me out.

That was a mile-marker, signaling a monumental shift. This was not the person I'd been married to for over a decade. It was a stranger, someone who had clearly checked out of paternal responsibilities. In that moment, I saw a glimpse of the fundamental change divorced men most likely experience when moving from a full family orientation to that of self-orientation. Three days later, Adam was released from the hospital fully recovered, but his new condition of asthma remained lurking in the wings.

On moving day, a team of smelly but strong men rang my doorbell at sunrise. Aldert took the day off from work to help haul boxes and my mother showed up to "watch the movers," even though I wasn't sure how helpful that was going to be. The moving men loaded two medium trucks up with pink-sticker items and by midafternoon pulled away from my fairy-tale abode. I turned around for a final mental snapshot. My happily-ever-after fantasies from across from the lake were gone. My throat tightened shut and my eyes welled up; I could barely stifle the emerging heartache.

Somehow these sturdy men shoved hundreds of pieces of furniture and boxes into the tiny new bungalow, utilizing the damp, unfinished basement as a warehouse. The kids came home from school, wide-eyed and curious about our new space. I'd been on autopilot for so long, I was totally ungrounded. My arms and legs were weak. I stood at the top of the basement stairs holding an open box marked "Adam's Toys: Legos." Alexandra called over my shoulder, "Mom, where are my pants and shirts for tomorrow?"

I turned my head to answer as my left foot slipped out from underneath me. I started moving in slow motion, face first toward the flight of hardwood basement stairs. I twisted my upper body, scraping the wall as I hurtled past the first narrow gray step. I released the box from my grip and tried to wrap my pinkie around the skinny railing, but my little digit was too small to stop the fall. I plunged headfirst, flopping down twelve hard wooden steps, cracking my elbow and knee and landing whiplash-style with my head against a cold cinder-brick wall.

Alexandra screamed, "Oh my God!" Aldert ran down the stairs chanting something in Dutch. I lay at the bottom, looking at my bloody, bent, nailless finger. I saw tiny bright square plastic pieces were everywhere and a baseball-size lump growing on my elbow. I had cuts in my leg, a tingling down my head, and my neck felt as if it were sticking out sideways. I reached up to touch the blood trickling through my hair.

I was injured but somehow managed to not kill myself. We probably should have called an ambulance, but as a staunch stoic, I convincingly mumbled, "I'm fine." Then I shakily climbed up the stairs with Aldert's help as my mother and three children stood there, gaping at me.

Aldert ran out to release the moving men and call a chiropractor for an emergency adjustment. I insisted upon taking a bath to soothe my jarred body and gingerly climbed another set of tight stairs to the tiny black mold-stained tub on the second floor. I carefully undressed, turned on the water, and crawled inside. The fall did more than twist and torque my body, it stripped me of my disguise. Tears burst forth like a tsunami, reaching down into the stuffed well of anguish beneath. I was consumed with a tidal wave of shame and remorse as I filled the bath with more tears. I was at my own funeral, mourning the simultaneous endings: my marriage, my beloved home, and my broken-down body. But mostly, I wept because my kids didn't understand. *Why did Mom do all of this to us?* I screamed at the bathroom walls, "You want to know how I am? I'm not okay! I'm not okay. I'm not okay." I sobbed even harder for the repressed tanks of sorrow that I had trapped inside.

Adam called up the stairs, "Dad is home from work and wants to know where we are." Clearly, he'd missed my stream of previous emails about moving day.

I hobbled around and moved in very slowly, unlike my traditional whirlwind style. Surprisingly, Rob didn't call or stop by for ten days. Most likely, he was too busy trying to find a last-minute residence and wallowing within his own vacuum of depression. Eventually, he located a condo six blocks away and started acting like a divorced dad, taking the kids every other weekend.

With the final lap of closure in sight, "divorce day" was scheduled for the following week. The actual divorce court process itself was startlingly simple; in fact, it took only five minutes. Both Rob and I showed up, stood next to our attorneys, and answered "yes" to three questions. Then the judge signed a piece of paper and shook our hands. We walked off and the marriage was dissolved.

Despite the easy legal resolution, when I returned to the bungalow, there it was again, rock bottom. I hit it, along with the cracking board of self-flagellation and the weighty misery of life-loathing. I climbed into bed, stared at the ceiling and faced my middle-age reality. I was forty-six, and upon adding everything up, it equaled zero: no house, no marriage, no current work, no acting projects, a pain-ridden body, and a RAV4 instead of a red convertible. If that isn't total failure, what is?

The mountain of change was overwhelming. I'd torn everything down to the ground and now I didn't feel like I had the strength to build it back up. I was convinced, *I can't do it anymore. I don't want to climb any more mountains. I don't want to be here.* I lay there begging the Universe to take me away. I was ready to see my lame life flicker out and get whisked to the "other side." I stayed in bed, completely still for two hours in complete surrender, but nothing happened. When I looked at the clock, it was 3:00 p.m. and I hadn't disappeared into the oblivion. So I got up out of bed, poured myself into the car, and picked up the kids from school, just like good moms do.

⁓ 21 ⁓

What You Resist Persists

The Universe acts like the Garden of Eden. Right when a person makes a courageous choice toward positive change, an opportunity wrapped in a colorful bow comes along. Are you "sure" you want something different? Are you really "willing" to stand up for yourself?

⁓

Meanwhile, Aldert had been in California working day and night for a demanding West Coast client. He made obligatory phone calls to me during his only time off, around 10:00 p.m. from the men's bathroom. Exasperated from his absence and lack of quality communication, I quipped, "I don't feel like I can open up to you while the urinals are flushing. It's disgusting! Why don't you just email me a weekly status report instead?" Through my experience with Jeff, I'd learned enough about healthy detachment to no longer fear endings. I didn't want to be with a man who was never around, so I said the four dreaded words, "We need to talk!"

Aldert flew home that Friday and drove straight to my house. This wasn't going to be a fun date. We walked to a quiet part of the beach and I lucidly explained, "You're a wonderful man, but we can't build a future if you travel for a living. I want a partner with whom I can share the daily ups and downs. I have to break up with you because being a 'road warrior' doesn't work for me."

He looked at me with despair, torn. Consultants miss rich family lives for urgent travel schedules and an excellent paycheck; that's how it works. Aldert was addicted to the "intellectual high" of his job; his smarts were the consumable commodity. On the other hand, he had had a loveless adult life because he was never home. He didn't want to quit, but even more, he didn't want to lose me.

The following week, Aldert bravely approached his boss and declared, "I need to get off the road." His superior was compassionate, but openly warned, "If you send this message out to the team, no one will want you in their consulting group. You're up for a promotion to senior manager and this might put a black mark on your record. In fact, it could end your career." Apparently, working in the same town where you reside was taboo.

Strangely, after Aldert expressed his need for reduced travel, the company tempted him with a shiny new penny. It was the chance of a lifetime: to work for nine months side-by-side with one of our country's billionaires in Seattle. This was the ultimate consulting Kool-Aid! Time and time again I've seen this happen. The Universe acts like the Garden of Eden. Right when a person makes a courageous choice toward positive change, an opportunity wrapped in a colorful bow comes along. Are you "sure" you want something different? Are you really "willing" to stand up for yourself? Can you say "no" to how things were in the past?

Aldert was distraught. He had a celebrated nine-month opportunity waiting for him across the country that would assuredly kill our relationship. He walked straight into the partner's office. "I really enjoy working for this company, but after four years of travel, I can't go to Seattle. I need to stay in Chicago." It looked like he was going to pass the metaphysical test.

The consulting partners were furious, flogging Aldert for noncompliance. They denied him a promotion and a well-deserved raise and refused to assign him to the next local project. Instead, to cool his jets even more, they gave him a dead-end back-office research assignment in the Sears Tower.

If moment-to-moment truth is the best process for living well, neatly "ending cycles" is also crucial for moving forward and ringing in the future. Aldert was trapped in a holding pattern, stuck between moving-on and misery. His typically bright and sunny disposition soured. He walked around with his head dropped between his shoulders, dejected and bored.

I challenged him, "How dissatisfied do you need to be before you change jobs? Why don't you use your gifted intellect to create an entrepreneurial business? I promise your courage will be rewarded!" In a country slipping into a gloomy economic pit, I had no business making such a promise, but I did it anyway. A few weeks later, Aldert walked in and quit. Somehow, he found the heroism to address his greatest fear: diving face-first into financial uncertainty.

Actually, my boyfriend did a better job of addressing his fears and patterns than I did. Some people take months to recover from separation, divorce, and moving, but not me. I wanted to appear invincible for the kids. I flatly refused to expose my hollow, raw side, the sad little girl who'd made it through a really tough year. Instead, I insisted on hosting a holiday dinner in the shoebox rental for sixteen family members and extended a good will invitation to Rob and Karyn. I utilized Christmas as an opportunity to prove to everyone that my down-sized modern family was not only good, it was better than before. *See, I'm not only fine, I'm thriving. Watch me, I'm a professional pretender and this is my show.*

Truthfully, after so many life-altering events, I was mentally and physically shattered. The more tasks I undertook, the more furiously I stewed inside and craved a break from the charade. But despite my feelings, I cleaned, decorated, put up the tree, shopped, and pre-pared an extensive home-cooked three-course meal.

I did however, give myself permission to take a lit-tle shortcut that would make the holiday season easier. I searched through the basement looking for re-gifting opportunities. I found an unopened build-it-yourself rid-ing stable complete with horses and jockeys, the perfect gift for my brother's young daughter. I also found a large scented candle for my mother, a wallet for Aldert, Match-box cars for Adam, and two pink scarves, one for Alexan-dra and another one for Emma. I wrapped everything up and checked these items off my list.

The dinner went off without a hitch. The meal was hot and delectable. Everyone enjoyed themselves, every-one but me. My ancient chains of overwhelm rattled and my attitude was atrocious. I wanted to run out of my own party screaming, "I hate Christmas; this holiday sucks! Everyone, get out of this revolting little house and leave me alone." But instead, I kept my mouth tightly shut and continued to play the role of gracious host even when Rob and his date were hours late.

The next day, I received a scathing phone call from my brother. "Did you know the stable that you gave my daughter had the name *Adam* printed across the top?" I was totally busted. My re-gifting was fully exposed. He was furious and foaming, "How could you do such a thoughtless thing?"

My face flushed with heat while I stammered, "I honestly thought she would like the stable. I had it in the basement and she likes horses. I'm really sorry. What can I do to make it up to her?"

My brother was so mad, he flooded the telephone line with retaliatory remarks. "Everyone in the family's afraid to tell you what they think of you, but I'm not. You've just ruined your life. Why didn't you work harder to save your marriage? Why am I the only 'normal' person in this family?"

I wasn't sure whether he was "normal" or not, but I was devastated. *Doesn't anyone understand I just moved, got divorced, almost killed myself falling down the stairs, and hosted the perfect dinner? Does re-gifting really make me such an awful person? Do I deserve a whipping right now?*

To make matters worse, the following week Aldert's parents flew into Chicago for a visit before their annual California jaunt. It didn't take long for their side comments to hit me like a ton of bricks. At first I heard a harsh reference to a Dutch cousin who was dating an "older" woman. Then, Aldert relayed a verbal slam about how the Moroccan maid thought that I'd trapped Aldert into supporting my children.

That was it! I snapped. I went on strike with all warring factions. If I were the Dalai Lama I might embrace my naysayers, but I am neither a prophet nor a saint. I was just a woman in the middle of a massive re-do.

I refused to communicate with my brother's family or with Aldert's parents until further notice. Going on strike might seem infantile for a grown person, but I wasn't sturdy or sound. I was too broken from the upheaval to take any more bashings. I cocooned for a while, licking my wounds. I also took in the persuasive words of John Welwood in his book *Perfect Love, Imperfect Relationships*. Welwood offers exercises that heal wounds of the heart and disengage us from the grievances we carry against ourselves, other people, and the world at large.

> What continues to fuel our grievance against other people is our aversion to the intense emotions—especially hurt, anger, and hatred—they trigger within us. Thus, to lay down our grievance and live at peace with the human race, or the person we live with, it's essential to make friends with these feelings. Learning to allow and open up space around the intense feelings and sensations in our body is a profound act of kindness that starts to melt down the ice of resentment that hardens the heart.
>
> —John Welwood, *Perfect Love,*
> *Imperfect Relationships*

I had a lot of ice to melt. The majority of my time here on Earth, I'd covered up my fiery emotions. But the content of this old adage remains highly accurate: Whatever we resist persists. Just as Welwood recommended, every night before I went to bed, I let my feelings have a voice and expand into space. I focused on the sensations of sadness, anger, and hatred without becoming carried away by the judgment or the stories that fueled them; I gave them room to be present. The techniques made me feel infinitely better and the hurt from the past fear, loss, and injustice seemed to dissipate. I met my emotions head-on and flatly refused to do anything that didn't feel good or to spend time with anyone who wasn't a pleasant, wholesome influence.

Stonewalling also offered me a couple of breakthrough lessons. It took me months, but while stewing in the sting of criticism, I realized I'd made a fundamental error: seeking support from family members who couldn't give me what I wanted. *What was I thinking?* I'd wanted my brother to honor and understand my choices, but he couldn't because of his traditional viewpoint. I'd also wanted Aldert's parents to embrace me as a daughter, but with our cultural differences, that probably wasn't possible. The minute I stopped feeling the *desire* for them to show me love in the form of acceptance, the thorny pain stopped. My patterns dissipated when I no longer craved a specific response. I moved to a place of compassion for those who had inadvertently hurt me. Through this exercise, I also embodied the second half of this rather ironic lesson: Love in the form of approval had to come solely from within. The only person who needed to approve of me, was ME.

Despite the fact that I had boycotted his parents, Aldert still loved me. He was on a mission to bring us closer and had a plan of his own. He announced, "Pack your bags. The two of us are heading downtown for a weekend getaway to the luxurious five-star Peninsula Hotel." We walked into the lush suite and he immediately dropped down onto one knee, opened a small square box, and proposed. I was blown away. Like a pirate, I grabbed the gorgeous two-caret square-cut diamond ring, admiring the sparkle.

Speaking from the experiences of a tremendously thorny year, I responded, "I love you and we can make incredible partners, but right now I'm not the 'marrying type.' I want to take this ring to symbolize our long-term commitment, but not necessarily as a date for the altar. Are you okay with that?" Somehow he looked relieved. Scheduling another milestone event wasn't an excellent idea until the dust from the divorce had settled. And quite frankly, the concept of marriage itself wasn't high on my list.

I gave Aldert an official "yes, but . . ." and we began a jubilant engagement celebration. That weekend, I experienced the happiest three days of my life. We were blessed with a fifty-degree winter day, the glow of true elation, fine dining, carriage rides, and the excitement of dancing the night away. I was overjoyed.

We arrived home, expecting that the news would be well-received. "Kids, we just got engaged. We want to build a life together, but we're waiting several years before we get married. And, Aldert will move in with us in May." To say that my young entourage was upset would have been an understatement. My superb mood and our celebration were trampled by new cycles of fits and silent treatments. But by now, I knew what to expect and I had the confidence that the kids would eventually adjust.

You Can Run, but You Can't Hide

I probably looked normal on the outside, but I was heading straight for a permanent wheelchair. How had I become a soft, weak blob, a midlife physical disaster? I was like the guy in the board game Operation. I had broken pieces all over my body and a group of medical professionals had to repair me with some tweezers.

~

For the most part, we quickly became a well-functioning, two-household divorced family. By early 2009, my children kept an open suitcase next to their beds and had adjusted to shuffling between the house and the condo. As predicted, the recession cut with a mighty blow, killing the job market, housing prices, and commercial acting opportunities. I had some cash from the house sale and felt lucky that I could coast financially for a while. To comply with my harebrained promises, I bought Adam a nerf pistol, Emma an eight-week-old Shih Tzu puppy, and my father helped sponsor the purchase of Alexandra's early high school graduation present, a Ford Focus.

I used my time during the day to revamp my corporate website, and another big opportunity came knocking on my door. An enthusiastic thespian-school mom invited me to help her resurrect the grade-school theater program. We would each select and direct a thirty-minute play of our choice. Even though I was an acting instructor neophyte, I loved the theater and working with grade-school kids and had some extra time on my hands. "Sure, I'm crazy about musical shows."

I chose a modern version of *Princess and the Pea*, and with nepotism alive and well, I cast both Emma and Adam along with eighteen other children. *How hard could it be?*

As with most big opportunities, there's something to learn that comes along for the ride. Parents in the high-rent district specialize in training their children to become competitive athletes and receiving services. Therefore, it shouldn't have been a surprise to me that no one was "available" to help with my production. I didn't realize when I signed on that I'd also agreed to be set designer, costumer, music director, choreographer, and prop and stage manager. Thank goodness one of the dads promised to build and paint the set. For that, I was tremendously thankful.

For six weeks, I showed up in the Parish Center with twenty kids and a coach's whistle to maintain order. The artistic teaching process was both difficult and satisfying. It was thrilling to watch a fully choreographed play unfold. Unfortunately, amid the craziness of running the production, I was also bombarded with endless emails, questions, and complaints from the parents. I started to feel like the ratty hired help, and this I did not particularly enjoy.

To make matters worse, at rehearsal one evening I pushed a large prop piece across the floor and felt a jagged stab of pain across my hips and calf. I fell to the ground with forty small eyes laser-beamed upon me. Something was seriously wrong with me.

Even though I'd kept physically active with the equestrian sport, my body issues had been looming on the horizon for many years: part of it due to genetics, another part due to aging, and the vast majority, pure neglect. I had sore heels from high arches and bad shoes, limited shoulder movement from halting horses and carrying young children, a twisted neck from the basement stairs, and now a spiky disk in my back.

Over the years, I'd tried a variety of alternative healing modalities. According to *The Secret*, people have experienced spontaneous physical healing from life-threatening cancer by watching funny movies and laughing their heads off. Well, I had experimented with hypnotism, energy healing, acupuncture, EFT (the art of tapping on meridian points), and watching a bunch of comedies. Unfortunately, none of these approaches seemed to provide me with long-term pain relief. *Fine, I'll go to the doctor.*

The orthopedic physician examined my twisted hips and diagnosed me with sciatica, traveling from hip to calf. I held out my arms so he could give me a strength test and evaluate my shoulders. He easily knocked my two sore extremities to the floor, stating matter-of-factly, "You have the arm strength of a newborn baby." He also suspected that I had plantar fasciitis in both feet. "Let's get some tests done, what do you say?"

I sat in a thundering MRI tube for hours and stood on cold metal plates for the foot X-ray machine. The news was ghastly. The doctor declared, "Dianne, you have a tear and a spur under your left rotator cuff. If you don't get surgery right away, you'll need a complete shoulder replacement within the next five years. The other shoulder has severe tendonitis. You have two compressed discs, one on the right side of your neck and the other on the left hip, which is creating the sciatica. And you have bone spurs on both heels."

I probably looked normal on the outside, but I was heading straight for a permanent wheelchair. *How had I become a soft, weak blob, a midlife physical disaster? I was like the guy in the board game Operation. I had broken pieces all over my body and a group of medical professionals had to repair me with some tweezers. What happened to me?*

According to Louise Hay's fascinating book *Heal Your Body A-Z*, pain and "dis-ease" are past patterns and trauma stored in the body.

> I have learned that every condition in our lives, there is a NEED FOR IT. Otherwise, we could not have it. The symptom is only an outer effect. We must go within to discover the mental cause. . . . The mental thought patterns that cause the most dis-ease in the body are CRITICISM, ANGER RESENTMENT and GUILT. For instance, criticism indulged in long enough will often lead to dis-ease such as arthritis. Anger turns into things that boil and bur and infect the body. Resentment long held festers and eats away at the self and ultimately can lead to tumors and cancer. Guilt always

seeks punishment and leads to pain. It is so much easier to release these negative thinking patterns from our minds when we are healthy than try to dig them out when we are in a state of panic or under the threat of a surgeon's knife.

—Louise Hay, *Heal Your Body A-Z*

Metaphysically, Hay nailed me on both accounts: Shoulder issues represent the ability to carry our experiences joyously, our tendency to make life a burden by our attitude. Lower spine issues represent the support of life, especially lack of financial support. Yes, I had many burdens and financial issues.

Although Hay recommended using new "mental thought" patterns to rid us of our ailments, positive ideas alone were not going to repair a ripped shoulder tendon. I needed good old-fashioned Western medicine. I canceled play practice for a week and agreed to endure the surgeon's knife to fix the torn rotator cuff. I also signed up for physical therapy to strengthen my weak lower back.

Aldert took me to the hospital in the early morning and picked me up hours later with four grisly bear cuts across my upper shoulder. I was hopped up on morphine and my left arm tightly bound in a black sling. I felt like I could fly.

A convalescent home would have been a smart choice because one-armed living inhibits most common activities. Single-handedly, it's impossible to open a box, jar, or envelope; pour shampoo; apply toothpaste; floss; hook a bra; pull up your underwear; or button a pair of pants. But I was on a tight budget and all I could afford was Aldert, my male orderly. He dutifully laid out six bowls, filled them with multicolored antibiotics, prescription and non-prescription pain meds, and sleep aids. He organized my pillows into the shape of a comfortable corral. He helped me locate giant sweatpants and an old sweater big enough to fit over a sling and also agreed to open anything I pointed at.

Not realizing shoulder surgery is one of the most challenging and longest physical recoveries, I was in mind-altering pain for weeks. I sat like a zombie watching reality TV, strapped to the Ice Man, a machine that pumps freezing water. I survived thanks to a synthetic opiate coma induced by Tramadol. Now, I understand how people get addicted to pain meds. Tramadol felt like hot chocolate pudding, viscously pouring through my veins. *There goes my mind, floating around in outer space.* For three hours I felt delightfully euphoric until the unfortunate morbid crash back into reality.

I also went to see Lisa, a highly recommended physical therapist. The minute I walked in, she laid her bony fingers on my fresh new wounds and rubbed hard in a circle. I yelped, "That hurts!" and jumped back away.

Lisa looked at me deadpan, and ordered, "Sit down and let's continue." She hooked up a set of pulleys over my head and told me to move the handles up and down thirty times. *Is she crazy? Doesn't she see I'm an invalid?* Lisa didn't care. "The body responds to repetition." She commanded, "Give me thirty reps."

I inched the pulley handles back and forth, hissing at her. Then she made me lie on the floor and I punched my little chicken arms up and down in the air. Considering the lack of tone and recently cut tendons, even the simplest movement was agonizing. Lisa switched to my lower back. "Push the small of your back into the table and hold it down while tapping your feet up and down thirty times."

I tensely fought back, "What are you talking about? I can't do that!"

Lisa callously responded, "Alright, then. It takes some people a while to figure out where their abdominal muscles are. Practice at home and we'll try again here next week." I left the clinic with my skeletal system screaming. I wrapped myself in the arms of the Ice Man and filled my stomach with more drugs.

I saw Lisa three days later and gave her a detailed list of my throbbing aches from our previous session. She just stared at me. This frigid, unfeeling woman never once uttered the words I longed to hear, "I'm sorry I'm hurting you." It wasn't in her job description. She made notes on the chart and gave me more exercises.

Repairing my body was going to be a huge feat both mentally and physically. Clearly, I was in no condition to direct a play, but the kids had already invested six weeks of time, so I had to finish what I started. I showed up the following week at practice with my trusty whistle, a sling, and a pocket full of pills.

While driving on my way to a post-surgical checkup ten days before the show, I received a devastating call. The father responsible for building our set had decided to bolt; he was "too busy." I almost hit the car in front of me. The Queen of Burden along with her lovely sister, Zero Support, filled me with anguish. Not only did I have to accomplish the impossible, I walked alone.

I was a handicapped volunteer mom "single-handedly" managing twenty kids in a school theater program. If Hay had been sitting in my car, she would have pointed at my pain-ridden body and said, "There it is, exactly what you NEED, a lack of emotional support, feeling unloved, stuck in a complete physical mess." And, I probably would have dumped the short blonde on the side of the road.

I pulled the car into a random driveway and called Aldert. Boiling with sentiments of injustice and on the verge of cracking up, I demanded, "You've got to help me. I NEED you to make the set." My fiancé told me to calm down and agreed to build our set over the weekend; there truly was no one else for the job.

Somehow, the set got constructed, costumes and props organized, and the kids acted to perfection. The play was a huge success throughout the entire school system. I should have been proud, overjoyed, glowing. Instead, I felt like the kid who made the winning goal and only got an "atta girl." I wanted more. I invested everything in this thankless backyard production. *Where was my recognition and giant bouquet of flowers?* I stewed for weeks, swearing I'd never contribute to the school again.

But over time, I realized this lesson was mind-bogglingly similar to the one I'd experienced over the winter. I was the Unsung Hero, seeking approval in the form of external recognition. Just like making Christmas dinner after moving and crashing down the stairs, I desperately wanted the school parents to appreciate me for my creativity and physical investment while being injured. Wrong! Directing the kids and enjoying the process had to be enough, all by itself. External acknowledgment was not the goal. The bell once again rang loud and clear: Acknowledgment and satisfaction had to come solely from within.

The play also highlighted another important issue, my sense of belonging. I finally accepted that I was a misfit in my own community. I didn't take the kids to the Bahamas on spring break. I didn't have a million dollars and I wasn't arrogant or entitled. I had a different paradigm. My joy came from adventure, theatrical expression, and living out on a limb. In the future, I would need to seek others to better reflect my uniquely metaphysical light.

I also realized that after months of hard work, Lisa was right. I didn't care for her personality, but the body does respond to repetition. There was no way I'd allow myself to be saddled to a wheelchair before my time. I committed to rebuilding my physical form. I would do whatever it took including bridging, crunching, toe-walking, and squatting myself into fitness. For over a year, I faithfully attended physical therapy and joined a health club so I could practice yoga twice a week.

~ 23 ~

The Bounty

In retrospect, the past decade was an organic voyage, each event emerging without structure or order. I took the roller-coaster ride from middle income to wealth to poverty, from fat to fit, from a mountain of lies to truth, from a broken body to strength, and from a loveless connection to standing side by side with a soul mate.

~

The time for Aldert to move in was upon us. Now, I'd like to report that everything was bubbly and smooth, but that's for fantasy novels and this is a real story. He shoved his massive belongings into our scrunched abode and rammed his desk into my pint-sized home office. Our claustrophobic living quarters looked like an army barracks and the basement a furniture jungle. The move-in also sparked another issue, namely, Aldert's exacting nature and his adjustment to living with three children.

I have three amazing, intelligent kids, but they're needy. They don't mean to be, but they are: "Mom, I'm hungry. Adam is copying me. I can't find my shoes. There are ants in the cat's food. I left my science book in the locker at school. No one invited me to the dance. The dog won't take a pee. We don't have the right jelly." This goes on from dawn till midnight.

I'm comfortable with the chaos because I have a free-flowing style. Aldert, on the other hand, grew up in a strict Dutch, spotlessly clean household where no nonsense was tolerated. He had lived his entire adult existence in apartments by himself. To top it off, he was sitting in our now comingled domicile day after day, searching for independent work projects in a sagging economy. It was a bad formula.

After living with us for one week, Aldert started shaking his head when he found empty potato-chip bags on the floor. He moved to grumbling while lifting abandoned toy cars off the couch. He grimaced and growled while wiping sticky, spilled juice from the kitchen floor. And, he advanced to using swear words when the girls left the front door wide open. Eventually, he just walked around constantly yapping orders, demanding that the kids keep the place orderly. Even Adam complained, "Mom, we don't like Aldert anymore. He was nice, but now he's mean. When you leave, he fusses at us the whole time."

I didn't see this coming. We clearly had "Odd Couple" management styles. I felt a spear of disappointment hit the bottom of my heart. *Where is my idyllic blended family? This is not what I expected post-move-in.* Our picture-perfect union was heading south.

I attempted to help Aldert adjust by inviting him to be fully expressed. "I've noticed you seem tense and crabby lately. How's the move going so far?" He immediately started to rant. "When the kids stay here, the house is a mess. I have to walk around all day picking up toys and trash. This never would have happened when I was young. My parents would have kicked me across the room. Plus, your kids don't feed or walk the pet and they waste electricity. I'm going to make a spreadsheet of duties and they'll have to check every item off the list or face the consequences!"

I sat there, listening to him carry on in disbelief. My kids had excellent grades and were highly functioning in and out of school. I'll admit the girls were a bit "cool" to him overall, but I was overjoyed that they'd adjusted beautifully to our new model. I wasn't concerned about wrappers and light switches. My brain filter heard, "I hate your kids and you're a shoddy mother."

I chided, "Why don't I just line them up and give you a big stick so you can beat each of them into submission?" He didn't appreciate my comment. Aldert was trying to tell me he had his own set of rules and wanted more respect for his vision. I felt myself pulling away. Maybe this move-in thing was a rotten idea.

We not only had to adjust to our smother-tight abode, but the Universe had more surprises for us: a series of new endings everyone had to face. After the puppy arrived, our twelve-year-old terrier developed a serious case of senior dementia and became hyper-aggressive, to the point of hanging off the mailman's leg. The dog was determined by the village to be not only "crazy" but "unsafe"; I had to make a choice to either put him down or face a county judge and harsh legal charges. I felt horrible, but I chose the first option. The kids were devastated.

Not long afterward, the new puppy developed bloat, gaining double his weight in fluids around his stomach and whimpering in distress. The vet drained the dog's abdominal cavity, but the bloat came back with a vengeance.

After two thousand dollars in diagnostics, the animal was found to have digestive organ failure and I had to put him down, the second animal in less than six months. Adding to our sorrowful year, the fifteen-year-old cat started having seizures and passed away owing to renal failure.

But that wasn't all. To make matters even worse, Rose, my ten-year-old horse, developed an inoperable bone cyst on the knee, rendering her permanently lame. I anguished and stressed. Not only did I love this animal but she was trained to perfection. I tried every possible medical and alternative healing treatment to reduce the growth, but nothing worked.

One day after walking Rose around the arena for exercise, I tied her up in front of her stall, something I'd done a million times before. I bent over to brush her leg and . . . *crack!* This gentle creature cow-kicked me with full force in the head right above the eye. I fell to the ground. A softball-sized lump grew on my forehead within seconds. The knot filled my entire palm and my eyeball swelled shut. Somehow, I managed to put the horse in the stall and drove myself home. The kids shrieked when Quasimodo walked in the front door. I looked like a domestic violence victim who'd had her head smashed against the dashboard.

Fortunately, I didn't have a broken head bone, but even the best makeup couldn't hide the small coconut-sized lump and double indigo black eyes. For two months, I canceled auditions and was required to explain the situation to my clients so they wouldn't call the police. It took a hoof-blow to the head for me to close the door on our final animal. I called Mel and he recommended a woman with an enormous private stable for the horse's permanent retirement and I swiftly gave our splendid young mare away.

For the next two years, our family bobbed on the waves of change, financial stress being at the core of the water's riptide. Both Aldert and I floated between feast and famine, finding regional consulting projects and searching for new ones. I went back into conservation mode, purchasing only essentials. If it wasn't on sale at Target, we didn't buy it. We lived in diligent frugality, but this time it was without the sense of panic; somehow, I knew we'd recover.

Rob too hit rock bottom. He broke up with his girlfriend and sat in his condo for over a year with no work or income. To start fresh, he decided to move to Arizona. He loved the Southwest, the heat, and the chance to explore new social relationships. Unfortunately, he stopped making child support payments, officially making him a "deadbeat dad" for a full year. This too added tremendous stress to my mind and our highly limited cash flow.

Yet, the most amazing part was, that with time and patience, our inventive blended family found harmony. We put structure into the household with a strict set of rules and extra "chore hours" for any child who "forgot" to clean up their mess. Aldert grew into a family man and learned to be less obsessive and compulsive, accepting daily life with disorder, carpooling, play dates, band concerts, and sideline cheering at football games. Miraculously, he also manifested the ideal consulting job opportunity with local work, regular hours, and lots of career development opportunities.

I too had some successes. I managed to become a frequently booked union indie film actor in Chicago and won multiple international MarCom Awards for client projects, this being an accolade I tremendously appreciated. I also grew and learned how not to take things personally, as Ruiz strongly recommended. Plus, Aldert's parents and I worked hard at establishing a happy, highly functioning relationship, which is now peaceful and caring. Also, I practiced truth-telling with my brother's family, doing my absolute best to express my feelings in the moment instead of letting my chains get rattled.

As for the children, our little bungalow offered ample access to schoolmates running in and out of its friendly yellow door. All three kids adjusted superbly well emotionally, socially, and academically, consistently hitting the highest honor rolls. Plus, a shelter pup and kitten added buoyancy and lightness to our household, as pets often do.

I directed two more school plays and coached the junior high cheerleading squad. Although I'd like to report that I turned two deaf ears to the intrusive parents, that wasn't the case. I frequently found myself as a rebel in hot water fighting both the PTO and parent athletic committees on several issues, but regardless of the situation, I picked up the phone and spoke my truth directly. I was honest, clear, and not seeking external validation or acknowledgment. The school children became my joy and I cherished the opportunity to watch them perform their little hearts out.

According to Jeff Brown, *Soulshaping* is about emerging:

> Growing is all about leaps into the seemingly unknown. Before you can find your way home, you must linger in the place of not knowing. Stay here until the next step organically arises. Sit until the questions that need to be

lived show themselves. By surrendering to the unknown, you create the space for a deeper knowing to emerge. Befriend your confusion.

—Jeff Brown, *Soulshaping: A Journey of Self-Creation*

I'll be honest, I'm not sure I can ever readily befriend my "confusion." I stumbled onto each road, bruising my knees and shins along the whole rocky path. I don't like to work that way. I would have preferred an organizational plan or system to help me revamp and make sense of the "unknown."

In retrospect, the past decade was an organic voyage, each event emerging without structure or order. I took the roller-coaster ride from middle income to wealth to poverty, from fat to fit, from a mountain of lies to truth, from a broken body to strength, and from a loveless connection to standing side-by-side with a soul mate.

After years of massive rebuilding in the dense fog, I'd incorporated "The Shortcuts for Living Well," absorbed many indispensable lessons, and was living in integrity, truth, and pursuit of my passion. Yet one item still remained undone. How was I going to fulfill my mission?

The wiper blades squeegeed an open a spot on the murky windshield. Finally, my mission and life's work had become crystal clear; I understood the intrinsic direction that I needed to take. The answer lay in my story: I wanted to help others find and achieve their greatest good by creating a *sanctuary for midlife transformation*. This would allow a full blooming of my unique natural skills, a blending of writing, performing, educating, and acting.

It took some diligent focus, but I went back to writing my chronicles every day. I put an hourglass on my desk and continued writing until the sand ran out. I also mapped out an interactive business, Live Your Everything, to help lighten the load for others by offering a path for personal reinvention.

I'd approached every change as a free fall, diving through the air and grabbing at Brass Rings along the way. I'd made more mistakes than I could even count, but I also absorbed the often difficult yet innately valuable teachings. I continued to sort through the debris, throwing out the bad, organizing the good, and eventually pulling my own body out of the smelly heap of upheaval.

Now, I had what I wanted all along: emotional peace, love, a uniquely sculpted family unit, an outlet for my creativity, and a new life in hand. By the way, this was the picture Sonia painted for me on my thirty-eighth birthday. It just took me over a decade to erect the living model from the shadows.

The most outstanding part of the journey was that with each and every step I felt happier. Isn't that what every parent says they want for their kids . . . to be happy? If someone asks me today the ultimate test question: "Do you love your life?" I can honestly say that the answer is "yes."

Bibliography

Benedict, Mellen-Thomas. "Near-Death Experience: Story of Mellen-Thomas Benedict, Journey Through the Light and Back." 2007. *http://www.mellen-thomas.com*.

Borysenko, Joan. *Fire in the Soul*. New York: Hachette Book Group, 1993.

Braden, Gregg. *The Divine Matrix*. Carlsbad, CA: Hay House, Inc., 2007.

Brown, Jeff. *Soulshaping*. Berkeley, CA: North Atlantic Books, 2009.

Canfield, Jack. *The Success Principles*. New York: HarperCollins, 2005.

Deida, David. *Intimate Communion*. Deerfield Beach, CA: Health Communications, Inc., 1995.

Gray, John. *Men Are from Mars, Women Are from Venus*. New York: HarperCollins, 1995.

Hay, Louise L. *Heal Your Body A-Z*. Carlsbad, CA: Hay House, Inc., 1998

Harramein, Nassim. *The Black Whole*, dir. Janice Jensen, Louisville, Co: Gaiam Entertainment, 2011. DVD, 93 min.

Hendricks, Gay, and Kathlyn Hendricks. *Conscious Living: Finding Joy in the Real World*. San Francisco, CA: HarperCollins, 2000.

Hicks, Esther, and Jerry. *The Vortex*. Carlsbad, CA: Hay House, Inc., 2009.

——. *The Law of Attraction*, transcription of Tape AB-2. San Antonio, TX: Abraham Hicks Publications, 1994. Originally recorded in 1988 by Abraham.

Levenson, Michael R., Carolyn M. Aldwin, and Loriena Yancura. *Explore: The Journal of Science and Healing*. Vol. 2, No. 6. Philadelphia, PA: Elsevier, 2006.

Lipton, Bruce. *The Biology of Belief*. Carlsbad, CA: Hay House, Inc., 2008.

MacLaine, Shirley. *Dancing in the Light*. New York: Bantam Books, 1985.

McTaggart, Lynne. *The Intention Experiment*. New York: Simon & Schuster, Inc., 2007.

Roth, Geneen. *When Food is Love*. New York: Penguin Group, 1992.

Ruiz, don Miguel. *The Four Agreements: A 48-Card Deck*. Carlsbad, CA: Hay House, Inc. 2001.

The Black Whole, dir. Janice Jensen, Featuring Nassim, Haramein, Gaiam Entertainment, 2011. DVD.

Vanzant, Iyanla. *Living through the Meantime*. New York: Fireside, 2001.

Welwood, John. *Perfect Love, Imperfect Relationships*. Boston: Trumpeter Books, 2006.

Whitfield, Charles L. *Healing the Child Within*. Deerfield Beach, CA: Health Communications, Inc., 1989

Zimberoff, Diane. *Breaking Free from the Victim Trap*. Issaquah, WA: Wellness Press, 1997.

About the Author

 Dianne Bischoff James graduated magnum cum laude from Northwestern University with an MS in Integrated Marketing Communications and has a BA in Psychology from Marquette University. In 1995, she launched Core Marketing Solutions, a branding consultancy located in Chicago and received both Platinum and Gold MarCom Awards in honor of corporate branding excellence. Despite her business success, Dianne felt great personal unrest. At forty, she embarked on a journey to find her heart and reignite a childhood passion for the dramatic arts. In 2003 she kicked off an acting career on the community theatre stage and over the course of eight years became a SAG-AFTRA union actor with numerous film, television, commercial, and industrial credits. At age forty-five, she began writing *The Real Brass Ring: Change Your Life Course Now!* In keeping with her entrepreneurial spirit, in 2012, Dianne also established Live Your Everything, a company that offers products, services, and resources to support the path of life reinvention and personal

transformation. Dianne currently resides in a suburb of Chicago with her three children and fiancé and enjoys adventure sports, hiking, boating, yoga, art festivals, and dance. Visit Dianne online at: *www.liveyoureverything .com.*